GUERRILLA
MARKETING

with

Adobe®
PhotoDeluxe®

Business Edition ■

GUERRILLA MARKETING

with

Adobe®
PhotoDeluxe®

Business Edition ■

 Kate O'Day & Linda Tapscott

with Jay Conrad Levinson's
Guerrilla Marketing International

Library of Congress Catalog No.: 98-89276

ISBN: 1-56830-486-2

2001 2000 99   4 3 2 First Printing: January 1999

Published by Adobe Press, Adobe Systems Incorporated, San Jose, California.

Adobe Press books are published and distributed by Macmillan Computer Publishing USA. For information on Adobe Press books address Macmillan Computer Publishing USA, 201 West 103rd Street, Indianapolis, Indiana, 46290 or visit Macmillan's World Wide Web page (http://www.mcp.com).

Part Number: 90015261 (1/99)

For Brendan, Seamus, and
Brigid—go raibh maith agat
—Kate O'Day

For Bill who makes me laugh
at the nonsense
—Linda Tapscott

Contents

Contents continued...

Contents continued...

How to...

The Basics *1*

Evolving into a guerrilla

Creating a marketing plan

At first glance, this book may seem to be aimed exclusively at small business owners, and in fact that is its main audience. But, if you're the owner of a Fortune 100 business, or the VP of marketing at Gump's, this book is for you, too. The reason: guerrilla marketing isn't a set of esoteric tips and tricks—it's an attitude. And Adobe PhotoDeluxe Business Edition is the tool you need to develop that attitude.

Flyers are perfect for simple and economical everyday advertising

Why guerrilla marketing?

Twenty years ago, during the reign of classical brand marketing, standard marketing philosophy consisted of buying national advertising, running ads, and sitting back to wait for people to buy your product. And it worked too, for a while. Consider the success of companies like Procter & Gamble and Johnson & Johnson. Today, however, consumers are more skeptical, there's more product competition, and mass media is fragmented. These changes set the stage for a new marketing approach—enter the guerrilla.

Becoming a guerrilla

To become a guerrilla, you don't need to dress in camouflage, drive an unmarked tank, or live in an underground bunker. All you have to do is care about your customers and want to run a successful business. You'll know that someone is aligned with the guerrilla philosophy when you see marketing that incorporates the following characteristics.

Every
marketing
plan must
cover
seven
critical
elements.

Self-seal mailers provide lots of space on one folded sheet of paper

4

The Guerrilla Manifesto

In order to sell a product or service, a company must establish a relationship with the consumer. It must build trust and rapport. It must understand the customer's needs, and it must provide a product that delivers the promised benefits.

The marketing focuses on impact rather than volume. Better a message that reaches 10 people who need the product and are ready to buy, than a message that reaches 100, not one of whom is interested in the product.

The marketing centers around benefits. The choice of product, the delivery, the service, and the advertising are obsessed with one thing—how does this benefit the customer?

The marketing recognizes the importance of positioning. Guerrillas understand that it's foolhardy to challenge marketing leaders on their own turf. Instead, they maneuver around the leaders, carving out their own marketing niche. Before you even begin to think of a business name, make sure you can recite your positioning statement in one succinct sentence.

The marketing stays around for the long haul. Guerrillas are committed to their plan and understand that results don't happen overnight. By setting goals and sticking with them, guerillas deal with the inevitable setbacks and stay on a sometimes rocky path knowing that failure is inevitable if you give up too soon.

Business cards often create that lasting first impression

Why you need a plan

There's no getting around it—marketing involves risks. You can never tell how your ad is going to pull, how many people will come to your grand opening, or what type of word-of-mouth advertising you'll generate. Non-guerrillas often tend to deal with this uncertainty by ignoring it. They go along, investing money in marketing when business is good and cutting back when sales go down. When an ad doesn't provide immediate results, they kill it right away. If an ad is effective, they get tired of it and go on to something else. While this laissez-faire approach is a plan of

sorts, it's not one designed to minimize stress and maximize profits.

Guerillas, on the other hand, recognize that a well-thought-out marketing plan is the key to success. First of all, a plan lets you focus on your ultimate goal and makes it easier to absorb the typical marketing ups and downs. Equally important, a plan helps you communicate your vision to your employees, your ad agencies, and your investors.

Writing a marketing plan

Every marketing plan must cover seven critical elements. The time you spend mulling over and defining these ele-

Understanding positioning

The concept behind positioning is simple—find a hole and fill it. Because of the tremendous information overload that we're all exposed to every day, most people find one or two attributes that they associate with a product. When they need those attributes, they remember the product. For example, Lexus, Mercedes, and Cadillac have cornered the market on "status" cars. If you want status, you go for one of them. Volvo, on the other hand, has nailed the "safe car for families" niche, not because of any unique production innovations, but with the application of smart marketing techniques.

The single biggest reason guerrillas fail is because they don't find a marketing niche. Once you've defined your niche, back it up with conviction. Every aspect of your marketing plan should reflect this niche and the unique way your company fills it. Positioning without substance never works in the long run.

Logos provide a quick visual identification of your company

ments now will pay off handsomely as you move toward marketing your product or service and creating advertising and media strategies.

Step 1. Identify the benefit to customers

To succeed, a product must offer a benefit that's greater than the product's cost. Ask yourself what people want, then make sure you distinguish between what you want and what your customers might want.

Postcards are a great guerrilla weapon for sale notices, grand opening announcements, invitations, and reminders

KERRY FAMILY CHIROPRACTIC

free!
Back care for one month!

Bring this card to our office and enter our contest for one month of free back care classes.

555-BACK

To succeed, a product must offer a benefit that's greater than the product's cost.

Evolving into a guerrilla

7

Step 2. Determine what business you're in

Your mission is to identify a genuine consumer need that will be filled by your service or product. Write down a description of your product or service and then list the features and benefits. How is your product different from the competition? If no unique feature or benefit jumps out at you, how can you compel consumers to switch to your product?

Step 3. Decide who the product is for

Once you've defined the product's benefits, you're well on the way toward identifying your target market. Begin to define the market segment by asking, "Who wants this product the most?" Test out your thinking by sitting down with a dozen members of the target audience and asking questions. You might have to do this several times. Then use this feedback to write a one-or-two sentence marketing statement that enunciates what you're offering and who you're offering it to.

Step 4. Devise an advertising strategy based on positioning

After you've defined the product and target market, delineated the competition, pinpointed the product's benefits, and differentiated your position from the

Consultants:

Flexible Pricing Packages

Personalized Planning

Full or Partial Services

Wonderful Weddings

Presentations provide the opportunity to meet with prospects and customers in person

Deciding how and where to spend your advertising dollars is an exciting job.

competition, you're ready to think about advertising. Always ask these two questions about any ad: What is the one idea the reader should get from this ad? What action should they take?

Step 5. Compute a budget

Every business has a natural rhythm where levels of sales and marketing are self-sustaining. You need to do enough marketing to stay in the game but not so much that you waste money. This is where a budget comes in. First, you need to figure out what percentage of sales you'll devote to marketing (10% is a good starting point). Then, find out what your competitors are spending and

budget for just a little bit more.

Step 6. Choose your tools

Deciding how and where to spend your advertising dollars is an exciting job. You get to research all different kinds of media: print, magazines, newspaper ads, classified ads, Yellow Pages, newsletters, inserts, point-of-purchase, trade shows, and lots more. Check out where your competitors are advertising.

Whichever venues you choose, PhotoDeluxe Business Edition has the templates and tools to help you quickly and easily produce professional, effective, and exciting marketing pieces.

Top 10 marketing secrets

1. Make a *commitment* to your marketing plan.

2. Think of that program as an *investment*.

3. Be sure your program is *consistent*.

4. Make your prospects *confident* in your business.

5. Be *patient* in order to make a commitment.

6. Become aware that marketing is an *assortment* of weapons.

7. Realize that profits come *subsequent* to the sale.

8. Run your company to be *convenient* to your customers.

9. Put an element of *amazement* in your marketing.

10. Use *measurement* to judge the effectiveness of your weapons.

Step 7. Implement a month-by-month timetable

After ranking the marketing tools that appeal to you, create a grid that you can use to plot your media plan, month by month. List the tool, the cost per use, the monthly frequency, and the monthly cost. Plan for an entire year in advance. If you've done your research and computed your budget, this step is the icing on the cake. When you're finished, you'll be well on your way toward reaching the pinnacle of guerrilla evolution. ■

Introductory offers are an excellent way to let clients take that all-important first step—the one through your door

Developing into a designer

Creating marketing materials

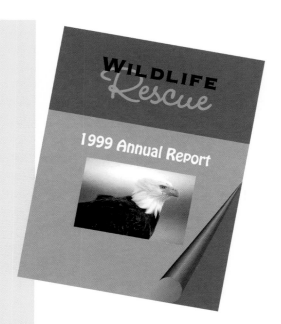

Even if you swear you don't have a creative bone in your body, you can create compelling marketing pieces using PhotoDeluxe Business Edition. The secret is in the easy-to-use, professionally designed templates. These templates, in conjunction with the fonts, photos, and clip art supplied on the PhotoDeluxe Business Edition CD-ROM, provide everything you need to become an instant graphics expert. There's no need to hire a designer or spend gruelling hours learning a graphics program. Simply choose a template and off you go.

Resizing and moving text

When you enter or edit text in PhotoDeluxe Business Edition, the text appears in a box with handles. To work with the text, do one of the following:

- To resize text keeping the same proportions, drag one of the corner handles.

- To change the width or height of text, drag one of the middle handles.

- To rotate text, drag one of the circles with the curved arrows inside.

- To move text, move the pointer over the text and when it turns into a black arrow, drag the text.

PhotoDeluxe Business Edition templates let you produce great-looking marketing materials in a matter of minutes

Learning PhotoDeluxe Business Edition

After you've installed PhotoDeluxe Business Edition, you might want to look at the tour movie (PDBEtour.avi), which demonstrates some of the interesting things you can do using PhotoDeluxe Business Edition. Once you start using the program, use the on-line help system to guide you through the product's features and benefits and to find out about specific tasks.

This book assumes you understand how to get photos into PhotoDeluxe Business Edition, add text, and get photos out of PhotoDeluxe Business edition. If you need help with any of these topics, see the Adobe PhotoDeluxe Business Edition Getting Started booklet or browse through the online help.

Using the Projects guided activities

All of the projects shown in this book were designed using PhotoDeluxe Business Edition. Most of them began with guided activities. Occasionally they use advanced features. The captions offer more information about each piece and detail which guided activities or special effects were used. At the end of each

11

Editing or adding text in a template

When you first start working with PhotoDeluxe Business Edition, you'll probably create most of your marketing materials using the templates. The quickest way to produce a piece is to simply add your photo or logo and replace the placeholder text.

To replace or change the content, color, or size of text:

1. Make sure the Object Selection tool is selected in the Selections palette.

2. Double-click the text to display the Text Tool dialog box.

3. Enter your own text.

4. Choose a new color by clicking on the Color box or choose a new size by typing in a new value.

To add text to a template:

1. Click the Text tool at the top of the window to display the Text Tool dialog box.

2. Enter the text and choose a font, color, and size. This box also lets you set the alignment of the text.

To delete text from a template:

1. Make sure the Object Selection tool is selected in the Selections palette.

2. Click the text to display the selection box.

3. Press the Delete key.

topic there is a how-to section that elaborates on a specific effect or illustrates how to adapt a template to create additional marketing pieces.

Previewing results

In most cases, you'll probably be printing your projects on your color printer. By default, the templates in PhotoDeluxe Business Edition appear with a white background. In actuality, this is a transparent background that shows what the piece would look like when printed on white paper. If you want to see what areas are transparent, you can change how the template appears.

To change the way the background appears in your documents:

1. Start PhotoDeluxe Business Edition and choose File > Preferences > Background.

2. Choose a small, medium, or large grid size.

   To change the color of the checkerboard squares, choose an option from the Set menu or click the color boxes.

3. Click OK.

To preview a template as it would appear on colored paper, simply create and fill a layer with the color. For complete

A busness card template, buscrd01, opened using the default background settings

The same document with the background preferences changed. Now the checkerboard identifies the transparent areas.

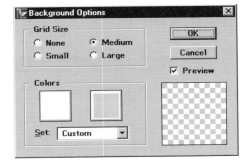

The background settings were changed to a medium grid, with a blue and white checkerboard

This is how the template looks when printed on white paper

This is how the template looks when printed on colored paper

instructions, see "Simulating your card stock" in Business cards.

Working with layers

While you're working in templates and simply changing colors or text, you don't have to concern yourself with layers. But once you feel adventurous enough to blaze a trail beyond the templates, you'll want to know about layers.

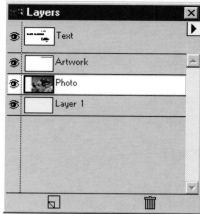

Layers are like clear sheets of plastic, stacked one on top of the other. Where a layer is empty, you can see through to the layers underneath. When you add a photo, pattern, color, or text to a layer, the filled space blocks what's on the underlying layers. The Text layer is always the top layer.

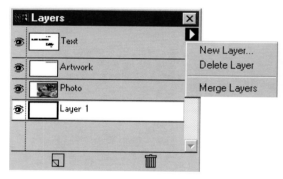

To select a command from the Layers palette, click the black triangle at the top right of the palette, then choose a command from the Layers menu.

14

Layers are designed to make it easy for you to change your mind. By putting things on separate layers, you can try out different combinations of colors, text, and graphics. Then, when you've made your final choices, you can delete the other layers. You never have to waste time re-creating something you've already done.

You can add layers, turn them on or off, rearrange their order, or delete them. There are a few exceptions:

• you can't delete Artwork or Text layers (although you can delete what's on them)

• all text goes on the Text layer

• the Text layer is always on the top of the Layers palette

To display the Layers palette:
Click the right mouse button and choose Show Layers.

When layers are used to create pieces in this book, a full explanation is provided in the caption.

Making selections

When you change a photo in PhotoDeluxe Business Edition, you affect the entire photo, unless you've made a selection. You can make selections based on color or shape. To make

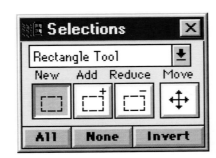

This selection was made using the Rectangle tool. The dotted lines outline the selected area.

*Clicking the Invert button on the Selections palette selects everything that was **not** selected. If you look carefully, you can see that the dotted lines are now around the head and around the edge of the photo. Everything but the head is now selected.*

Filling the selected area with color changes everything between the dotted lines. The unselected area is not affected.

Select
what you
want to
effect.

selections, you use the tools on the Selections palette.

To show the Selections palette:
Click the right mouse button and choose Show Selections.

The key to working with selections is to remember, "Select what you want to effect." You can tell an area is selected when it's surrounded by a dotted, moving marquee (sometimes called "marching ants").

When selections are used to create pieces in this book, a full explanation is provided in the captions.

Getting the most out of PhotoDeluxe Business Edition

There are no complicated procedures or rules for working in PhotoDeluxe Business Edition. The most important rule is to feel free to explore your creativity! But there are a few things that can help PhotoDeluxe Business Edition work at top speed and allow you to get more out of the program.

Keep your files small. Use the lowest resolution that works for the output you're using. See "About resolution" in online help for more information.

To check the file size before you open a gallery photo, click the thumbnail title

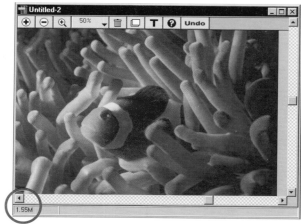

To find out how much memory the photo is using, check the value at the bottom of the PhotoDeluxe Business Edition window

16

◆ Let your imagination be your guide

◆ Know when you need to hire outside help

◆ Try out your ideas on helpful friends and family members

◆ Save everything until the project is finished (and then archive it)

Merge layers to save disk space and reduce file size. Be sure you're really done working with the image before merging layers. There isn't any way to "unmerge" layers. See "Working with layers" in online help for more information.

Assign more RAM to PhotoDeluxe Business Edition. Having more memory is particularly useful when you're working with large files and applying special effects. For more information, see "Allocating more memory to PhotoDeluxe Business Edition" in online help.

Keep as much free space on your hard disk as possible. Unless you change it, PhotoDeluxe Business Edition uses the hard disk where PhotoDeluxe Business Edition is installed as the "scratch disk." (A scratch disk is where the program stores working data and performs computations when there's no more room in RAM.) If you have another hard disk that's faster, or has more room on it, you can switch the primary scratch disk. You can also assign a secondary scratch disk. For more information, see "scratch disk" in online help.

Keep as
much free
space on
your hard
disk as
possible.

Turn off Clipboard export. If you're not going to be copying the PhotoDeluxe Business Edition documents into other applications, you can save space by not making the Clipboard available to other programs. To turn off this feature, choose File > Preferences > Export Clipboard. For more information, see "Copying a selection between applications" in online help. ■

Top 10 PhotoDeluxe Business Edition secrets

1. Explore your creativity.

2. Save often.

3. The more memory you assign to PhotoDeluxe Business Edition, the better.

4. Keep the file size as small as possible.

5. Don't increase a photo's resolution.

6. Use layers to try out different effects.

7. Use small strokes when using the painting and editing tools.

8. You can't work in advanced mode while you're in the middle of a guided activity.

9. Choose Help from the menu bar to get information on specific tools, commands, or projects.

10. Make sure the PhotoDeluxe Business Edition CD-ROM is in your CD-ROM drive before you try to access sample photos, clip art, or templates.

18

Your Business Identity   *19*

Logos

Presenting yourself symbolically

PlaySTORE
"Toys for Today's Children"

FINANCIAL CARE, INC.
DOWNTOWN

Your logo is a visual symbol that immediately identifies your company or product. Well, immediately that is, after you've used it for a while. Good logos take some time to get established, but then they usually remain for a long time. Think of the Energizer bunny, the Nike swoosh, the Gerber baby, or the Pillsbury dough boy. Well-designed logos equal instant recognition.

Logos
should
reveal who
you are
and what
you do.

A simple, straightforward logo can be very effective

What's a logo?

A logo can be anything from the way you print your name and address to a sophisticated full-color, professionally designed graphic. The idea is to get across your business identity and evoke an emotional response. Logos should reveal who you are and what you do. Use a logo to add a human dimension to your company and to let your company or product personality come through. A logo can display many aspects of your character: respectable, creative, whimsical, efficient, experimental, experienced, adventurous, and so on.

Choosing a logo type

In general, there are two kinds of logos, specific and quality. A specific logo is a visual way to position your company. Ben and Jerry's use of a cow, for example, implies the freshness and simplicity of their Vermont background. Apple Computer's rainbow apple is universal, clean, simple, and fun. It provides an extremely effective way for this company to stand out from the self-imposed seriousness and technological jargon that permeates the computer industry.

A quality logo uses an easily remembered symbol to reinforce the position-

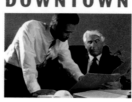

FINANCIAL CARE, INC.

DOWNTOWN

Using a photograph emphasizes the importance this company places on a personal relationship with clients

Tips for a typographic logo

- Start by setting the initials or name of your company in a variety of font sizes and styles. Notice where one letter might go into another or if the words or letters suggest an interesting or unexpected shape.

- Experiment with compressing or expanding the typeface or try mixing two typefaces. This is especially effective if your name blends two words such as "Playstore."

- Try boxing the type, using an underline rule, or reversing out part of the type.

ing done in advertising. It may have little or nothing to do with the company or it may refer to the company's name or product. The rings on the Audi logo, for example, don't have much to do with cars but do present an easily recognizable symbol of prestige. Snap, Crackle, and Pop do not really live inside a Rice Krispies box but they do an admirable job of making us think of (and even hear!) our morning cereal.

Quality logos are most effective for companies that advertise a lot. Through repetition and association, the logo comes to represent the product, even if the consumer doesn't read the entire ad.

Just the image of MacDonald's golden arches reminds us that a) we're hungry, b) it's time for a break, and c) french fries and a burger are just what we're longing for. That's a quality logo in operation; not only does it inform, it recalls the entire positioning of MacDonald's (fast, good, friendly, convenient) in a nanosecond.

BF Construction, Inc.

The interesting texture inside this company's initials helps to make this typographical logo particularly effective. The texture was created using the Special Effects > Elegant > Crackle guided activity.

Designing the logo

Before you make decisions about the design of your logo, ask yourself this question: "What qualities do you want to spring to the customer's mind when they think of your company?" This will get you started in the right direction.

Think carefully before you commit yourself to a logo. A business identity is more permanent than an advertising campaign and you'll be looking at your logo a lot, for a long time. In fact, you probably won't alter your logo unless your company undergoes a major change or the logo style becomes too dated.

Whether you decide to go for a specific logo or a quality logo, don't spend too much time worrying about telling a story. If you need to explain the significance of your logo, it's not doing its job. Always include your company name either in or under the logo. One recent survey found that less than 50% of brand products were instantly recognizable unless they included the company name along with their logo.

PhotoDeluxe Business Edition, with its wealth of photos and clip art, provides a fertile amusement park for you to explore when creating a logo. Take the

*Play*STORE
"Toys for Today's Children"

*Mixing typefaces
seamlessly blends this
two-word company
name into a single-word
logo*

time to play with elements of your letterhead, with different combinations of type, or with interesting combinations of text and graphics. Then try out the logo on friends and family to see if it receives the reaction you're hoping to get from your customers.

When designing the logo remember that it needs to fit and look appropriate in a lot of different places: on your cards, on your stationery and envelopes, on labels, on the Web, as part of your packaging, in print ads, on mailers, and so on. Create a logo that looks good big or small, reads well in color or black and white, and always makes you proud. ■

What shall we name the baby?

Before you can design your logo, you obviously need a name for your company. If you're going to stretch beyond your own name or initials and nothing comes immediately to mind, here're some naming tips:

- Let your name tell what you stand for. Make a list of your company's attributes, such as quick, reliable, unique, honest, fun, convenient, guaranteed, best, and so on.

- Decide if you want a generic, descriptive, or fanciful name.

  - Generic names immediately telegraph what your business is. They don't provide any positioning though (Stage Pros, BF Construction).

  - Descriptive names (a guerrilla's best bet) tell something about your product and yet are unique and easier to remember (Tasteful Catering, Harmony Music).

  - Fanciful names are fun but more difficult for customers to decipher (Get a Life!, "Just the facts, Ma'am").

- Give yourself a name with a positive ring. It should make people confident, enthusiastic, and eager to work with you.

- Don't let your name limit you. For example, Creative Lighting will not work if you decide to expand into other furnishings. Creative Chambers is more expansive.

- Pick a name that looks and sounds good: on your card, on the phone, on the Web, and in advertisements.

- Names created by committee usually don't work.

- Whatever you do, conduct a legal search on your name before you start using it. Very few guerrillas can afford lawsuits, especially when they're just starting out!

Fill text with a pattern

The Workshop Warrior logo uses the simple technique of filled text. Here's how to fill your own text with a pattern. First, choose File > New to create a file big enough to hold the text. Five inches by five inches will give you enough room to experiment.

Click Projects > Web > Title. Follow the guided activity to enter your text. Try out fonts until you find a wide one that you like.

When you get to the Fill step, click Selection Fill. In the dialog box, click Pattern, then click Next to cycle through until you find an appropriate pattern. This example uses the Nails pattern.

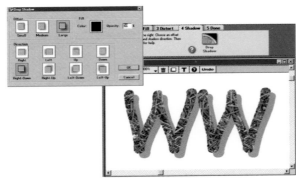

Adding a drop shadow makes the text stand out from the background. In the Shadow step, the shadow color was set to dark gray and the Large Offset and Right-Down options were selected.

If you want to increase the offset of the shadow from the text, use the Object Selection tool to select the shadow, then drag until the shadow is where you want it.

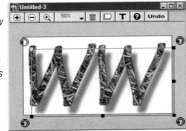

Note: *PhotoDeluxe Business Edition provides another way to create shadow text using Adobe Connectables. To try it out, click Internet > Internet > Guided Activities, then choose Shadow Text from the Other Activities menu.*

MARKETING TIPS

◆ Always include your name in or under the logo

◆ Don't make your logo so abstract that it's obscure

◆ Stick with the logo long enough to build brand recognition

◆ Put your logo on bags and boxes so that your customers advertise for you

Business cards

Creating a good first impression

One of the first things you do when you start a small business is acquire a business card. A card brings with it an instant sense of credibility, trust, and reliability. Ideally, it projects an image of who you are and what you do. For a small business, your card is most often the marketing tool that creates that all important first impression.

To be effective, your card should be part of your overall business identity. PhotoDeluxe Business Edition includes template families that allow you to create a matched set of cards, stationery, and envelopes. Take a look at your marketing plan and make sure your identity is aimed at the right market niche and target audience. Then, choose a template that radiates experience, concern, trust, and confidence.

Bypass the temptation to cut corners on your card. Run-of-the-mill cards can label you as unoriginal and unimaginative. Your job, as a guerrilla marketer, is to make your card stand out. An effective and dramatic card provides a major opportunity to distinguish yourself from the competition.

What goes on the card?

You have a lot of leeway when it comes to deciding what to put on your card. At a minimum, include your name, company, address, phone number, fax number, email address, and Web address. After the basics, you can improvise. Consider adding:

Anne Smith

17A Broadway Street Crossroads, AK 01234
Phone (123) 555-7777 Fax (123) 555-7778
www.petsittersinc.com

petsitters, inc.

Including portraits of pet clients turns template buscrd25 into an eye-catching and unusual card

Adding the tag "Life Insurance Specialist" turns template buscrd08 into a more distinctive card

Life Insurance Specialist

Westwood Insurance

Mary Smith

phone 123-555-1212

174 Broadway Street
Jonesville, PA 01234
fax 123-555-1213
www.westwood.com

- A tag line. The tag can be a positioning statement (The Best Dog Walker in Detroit), a slogan (Premiere Means Quality Produce), or a short description of your company (Specialists in Kitchen Remodeling).

- Frequently requested information. For example, list your hours or provide directions to your location. You can even include pricing information such as $35/hour or No Charge for Initial Consultation.

MARKETING TIPS

◆ Include a map on the back of your card

◆ Feature photographs of your products, office, or employees

◆ Include quotes or jokes that make your card amusing

◆ Create multiple cards for different audiences

Post your
cards on
bulletin
boards or
drop them
in the
mailboxes
of likely
prospects.

**Ever Green
Lawn Services**

Jack Bean

phone 123-555-1217
123 A Street, Centerville, WA 01234
fax 123-555-1219, www.lawnservices.com

*The interesting shape
of template buscrd19
makes this card
memorable*

• Information that provides a public service, such as useful 800 numbers, area codes, or Web addresses. Not only will you reap goodwill, you'll also guarantee that your card is looked at frequently.

Above all, be sure your card clearly explains what you do. It's amazing how often someone looks at a card and can't remember who gave it to them or what it was that they did.

Designing the card

PhotoDeluxe Business Edition makes it easy to produce creative, professional, and impressive business cards. You can choose from a large variety of templates designed for specific businesses, or you can express your creativity by modifying a template to meet your own needs. You don't need to stick to standard-sized cards. Try experimenting with double-sided, or fold-over cards, both of which give you more room for information and let you stand out from the crowd.

If you're a consultant, real estate agent, or travel agent, PhotoDeluxe Business Edition contains business card templates especially designed for your business. To use these templates, choose Projects > Business Guides, select your business, and then click Business Cards.

If your business doesn't fall into one of these categories, click Projects > Cards > Business Cards. Follow the guided activity to choose and customize a template by inserting photos, including clip art, or editing text.

If you prefer, you can use one of the templates as a jumping-off point for your own creative efforts. For more information on modifying a template, choose Internet > Adobe > Guided Activities > Edit a Template. Follow the simple steps to change the color and text on a business card template.

Printing your cards

Before you choose a template, consider the stock you'll be printing on. There are many types and colors of card stock available. You can print your card on white or buff paper

Coloring the discount information red makes it jump out from this modification of template buscrd07

The template as it would appear on white paper

The template as it would appear on colored paper

Simulating the card stock

The paper stock you use to print your cards has a huge influence on the color of type and graphics you choose. If you're planning on using colored stock, you can preview the appearance of the printed card. Click Advanced and then create a new layer. Click Effects > Selection Fill and choose a color that approximates the card stock. Move this layer to the bottom of the Layers palette. By creating several layers, and then turning them on and off, you can experiment with different colors. Don't forget to delete the color trial layers before you print!

Hand out
your
business
card at
every
opportu-
nity.

for a conservative look, or you can project more individuality by selecting bolder colors or a distinctive border. PhotoDeluxe Business Edition helps you find the stock you want by letting you browse the Avery catalog online. Simply choose Internet > Avery and then click the Avery home page. Return to PhotoDeluxe Business Edition when you're ready to create your card.

Business card stock is designed to print multiple copies on each sheet. To print your cards on Avery stock:

1) Choose Send and Save > To Printer > Multiple on a Page.

2) Click Type and in the Choose Paper Type dialog box, choose Avery for the Paper brand.

3) Choose the card type that you need, such as Laser Business Card, Ink Jet Business Card, or Photo Quality Business Card.

For more information on choosing and printing on Avery papers, see "Using Avery paper stock" in Labels.

Distributing your cards

Once you have your cards, be sure and hand them out at every opportunity! When you go to a meeting—bring your cards. When you go to a party—bring your cards. When you go on an interview—bring your cards. And always bring your cards (and leave them behind) when you call on prospects.

Try posting your cards on bulletin boards or dropping them in the mailboxes of likely prospects. Or, offer a discount if people present your business card at the time of a purchase. People need to know about your services before they can use them! ■

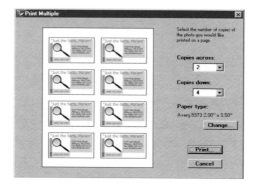

Choose Send & Save > To Printer > Multiple on a Page to save paper when printing your cards

Make a bookmark

You can easily turn a business card template into a bookmark.

This business card was created using the buscrd23 template.

Open your business card file and save it with a new name. If the Layers palette is not showing, click the right mouse button and choose Show Layers.

Choose Merge Layers from the Layers menu.

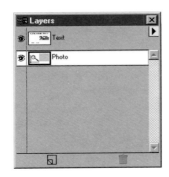

To make the business card long enough for a bookmark, click Advanced > Size > Canvas Size. In the dialog box, increase the width and click the middle left Placement box to add space to the right of the card.

Choose New Layer from the Layers palette and name the new layer background. Drag the layer to the bottom of the Layers palette.

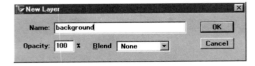

Fill the background layer with a color by choosing Advanced > Tools > Color Change. Add text wth the Text tool.

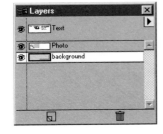

Stationery

Embellishing your name

Stationery, along with business cards, is one of the most frequently seen representations of your business identity. Whether you're writing a proposal, responding to an inquiry, or sending out introductory letters, your stationery often serves as the initial contact with clients. Make sure the impression they get reinforces the quality and professionalism you're striving for.

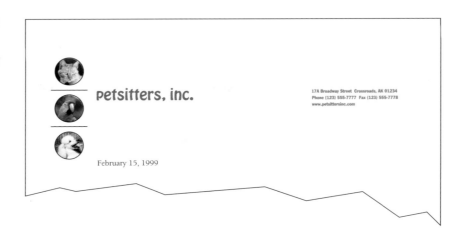

This letterhead places all the important information at the top of the page. When unfolded, all the information can be seen at a glance. This example uses the letter17 template.

Every business has stationery. This is both the good and bad news. It's good news if you're trying to find delivered-in-a-day stationery. It's bad news because you don't have many options when you use this cookie-cutter approach. Except in an emergency, take the time to design unique stationery.

Adding to the package

In most cases, you'll use stationery that complements and repeats the design of your business card. PhotoDeluxe Business Edition makes this easy by providing matching sets of templates for cards, stationery, and envelopes. If you modify a template, you can quickly replicate the change in the other templates.

At first glance, creating an interesting letterhead seems like an easy enough task. Of course your stationery will include your name, address, phone number, fax number, email address, and Web address. If you're required to display registration details for legal reasons (such as Incor-

If you'll be faxing the stationery

Many businesses use their stationery when sending faxes. If you plan to do this, choose a design that translates well into black and white. The design should not include text that runs over colored boxes or other any other elements that will appear as gray blocks in the fax. Check that the text is big enough and placed in a logical position for a fax heading.

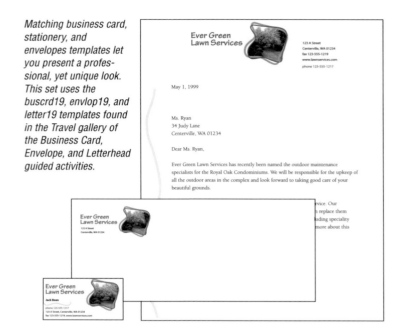

Matching business card, stationery, and envelopes templates let you present a professional, yet unique look. This set uses the buscrd19, envlop19, and letter19 templates found in the Travel gallery of the Business Card, Envelope, and Letterhead guided activities.

porated or Limited), be sure to include them in the letterhead design.

But these are just the basics. Be creative! Adding that special touch is where your guerrilla mentality serves you in good stead. At a minimum, include your logo and a one-sentence positioning statement. Beyond these simple additions, use your stationery to reinforce your uniqueness. Have you received a favorable review in a popular trade journal?

Personalize your stationery by including additional information, such as your board of directors. This stationery was created using the letter05 template.

DESIGN TIPS

◆ Choose white or buff for the background color

◆ Make sure the design works both when the letterhead is flat and when it's folded

◆ Group related information in visual units

◆ Include tags on the back of envelopes

Stationery

35

Try including a quote or the recognizable logo of the journal.

Moving beyond traditional

One simple trick is to use the left or right margin as an integral part of the design. You might rotate the text of your company name and run it down the side of the stationery or you can list the full range of services that you provide. Do you have an impressive board of directors? Why not list them in the margin?

Not all the information needs to be at the top of the page. Some stationery puts addresses or other information at the bottom. Nor does your logo or name need to be centered on the page; many designs put the information in the upper right or upper left corner. A more radical design might even include a name or other text in the letter section of the stationery. (This text is usually screened back so it doesn't interfere with the contents of the letter.)

Be sure to
include
your logo
and a one
sentence
positioning
statement.

Way Out Travel
Italy
136 Summer Street Riverview, KS 01234
Phone (800) 555-UFLY, Fax (123) 555-1213
www.wayouttravel.com

Way Out Travel
Greece
136 Summer Street Riverview, KS 01234
Phone (800) 555-UFLY, Fax (123) 555-1213
www.wayouttravel.com

Way Out Travel
Costa Rica
136 Summer Street Riverview, KS 01234
Phone (123) 555-1212, Fax (123) 555-1213
www.customtravel.com

February 8, 1999

Mary and Maureen Marble
124 Temple Place
Riverview, KS 01234

Dear Mary and Maureen,

As valued Way Out Travel veterans, we think we know you travel preferences and
needs quite well. That's why we're sure you'll be interested in the exciting, new,
backpacking vacation packages we will be offering in the spring.

COSTA RICA FOR $10 A DAY!

This is the trip you've been waiting for. With your sense of adventure and desire of
off-the-beaten-path travel experiences, we know you will love this relaxing 14-day
journey.

Call today and we'll send you our new brochure outlining the wonders of beautiful
beaches, unspoiled forests, and hidden gems of wonder Costa Rica. These trips are
fulling up fast, so be sure and call today.

Excitedly,

Joani

Joani
Travel Consultant

*Using templates makes
it easy to customize
stationery for different
target markets. This
example was created
using template letter18.*

While you want your stationery to make
a visual impact, it's also important that
people get the essential information at
a glance. When choosing a typeface and
color, be sure that the letters are large
and present enough contrast to be read
easily. Don't opt for a noveau or widely
spaced type that's difficult to decipher.

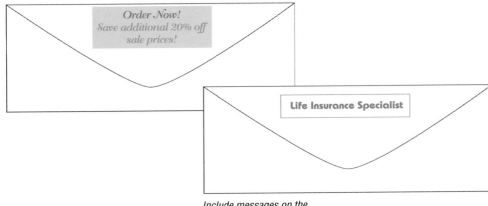

Include messages on the back of the envelope using clear or colored Avery labels. The back of the envelope may be the most important part since it's the first thing most customers see!

Remember to place related items together. No one wants to go searching around for a city, state, or zip code when all they're trying to do is address an envelope.

Don't forget the envelopes

Since the stationery design will be carried through on the envelope, keep a few things in mind when choosing the design. First, make sure the design looks good on a standard-sized envelope. If you're going to use an envelope with a glassine opening, be sure your design leaves enough space so that the typed address can show through the opening.

MARKETING TIPS

◆ Strive for a professional, yet unique look

◆ Include your logo and positioning statement

◆ List awards and other distinctions

◆ Use a photo of yourself to add a personal touch

◆ Create several stationery styles to reach different target markets

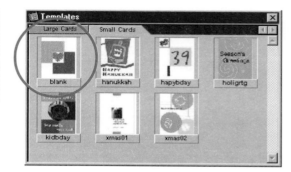

Create note cards that match your stationery

By using the colors and logo of your company, you can create note cards that carry on your business identity. Use these cards for hand-written invitations, thank-you cards, or personalized bon voyage notes!

Choose Projects > Holiday cards and choose a layout (this project uses the Single-fold Top fold layout). In the Style step, select the blank card template.

Add the photos or logo you want to use. You can also add photos on the back, top, or bottom of the card and add text as needed. Click Done to leave the guided activity.

Finally, don't overlook the back of the envelope. This is the ideal place to put a personal message or your positioning statement.

To add text to the back of your envelope, make and print a label (see Labels). You can print the label on clear stock or stock that matches your envelope for a more printed look or you can repeat your name and add a photo to the label. Stick the label on the flap and your important message is right where everyone is most likely to see it! ■

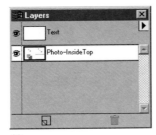

Before

After

To edit the colors in a template, first choose Merge Layers from the Layers palette.

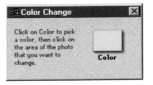

Click Advanced > Tools > Color Change to select and change the colored areas.

In this example, the purple area was changed to yellow to match the stationery.

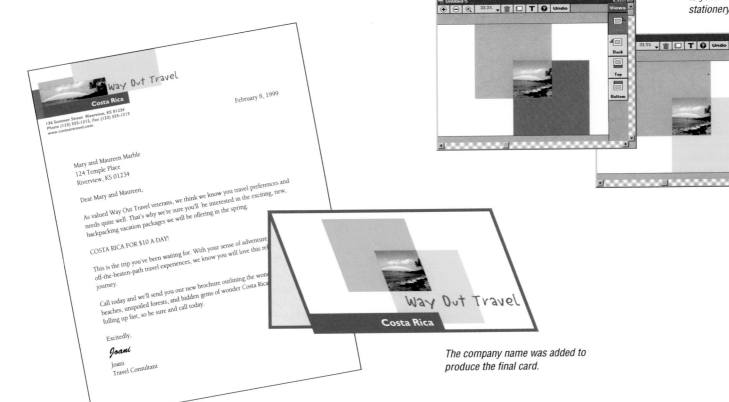

The company name was added to produce the final card.

Brochures

Providing detailed information

A s a typical consumer, you know that before you buy something (especially when that something is expensive), you want information. And, even though you might not realize it consciously, you also want reassurance. Most people are afraid of making a mistake or jumping into a deal too quickly. One effective way to relieve your customer's anxiety is to send or give them a brochure.

Brochures are the best way to provide detailed information and impart confidence in you and your product. At the same time, they are a powerful way to strengthen your business identity. Because it is so important, spend a little time thinking about what you want your brochure to accomplish before you design and write it.

A brochure gives your customers the chance to learn more about your company in an unpressured environment. Create a brochure that informs and explains, so that it's easier for prospects to justify spending their money. Use your brochure to gently break the ice and present the specific information needed to make an informed purchase. Don't expect the brochure to close the sale for you.

How much is too much?

Unlike advertisements or inserts, brochures aren't meant to grab attention or convey an instant message. Since the prospect has indicated an interest in more information, provide a lot of it. Feel free to expound on critical ideas or concepts. Answer important questions, even before they're asked. Take advantage of the opportunity to describe the features and benefits of your product with great precision. To make the brochure more than a sales tool, try telling the potential buyer a bit about yourself, share your business philosophy, and emphasize that yours is a quality business that cares about what you do and whom you sell to.

Don't be afraid to list your accomplishments. The prospect wants to know your experience with other clients. If you've won an award or received some other recognition, present it proudly. To show the prospect that they're in good company, list other major customers or buyers. And since nothing sells as well as personal recommendations, include testimonials. Remember,

The border on this brochure ties it to the company's business cards and stationary

Exotic Floral Designs

The beauty of the islands brought to your event...

We specialize in exotic and tropical flowers for any occasion.

Free Delivery!

Order by Phone!

Rush Orders Accommodated!

Magnolia, CA 12345
Phone (123) 555-1212

Brochures

41

A coupon on the back of the brochure gives the customer a reason to buy now or keep the brochure handy

the more information you provide, the more comfortable the prospect will feel buying from you.

If technical or performance data about your product will help make the sale, include tables or fact summaries. Your brochure needs to impress not only the buyer but also the potential user of your product.

Consider including reference material in your brochure, especially if it is information that your prospect will want to hold on to. For example, you can include useful phone numbers, schedules of upcoming events, hours of operation, or directions to your location.

Nothing scares away a prospect faster than an out-of-date, incomplete, or unfocused brochure. Create your initial brochure with care, and then review it periodically (when you're doing the yearly revision of your marketing plan is a good time). Make sure the information is always up-to-date.

Designing the brochure

A well-written, well-designed, and well-produced brochure lends credibility and professionalism to you and

For rapidly changing information

If your product changes often to keep up with evolving technologies, consider putting a pocket inside the back cover of the brochure. You can then insert updated sheets as needed. You can also use the pocket to include a price list.

Make sure the information in your brochure is always up-to-date.

Sunflower DayCare Center

Pricing Guide

NEWBORNS TO 1 YEAR OLDS
2-4 hrs a day..............$200
4-8 hrs a day..............$300

2 TO 4 YEAR OLDS
2-4 hrs a day..............$100
4-8 hrs a day..............$200

Additional hours on care after 6PM, add 20%.

Field trips and computer classes included in the monthly fee.

Special meals available upon

your company. It conveys a quality image that demonstrates that you're serious about what you do. Whether you design the brochure yourself or decide to hire a professional designer, make sure you feel comfortable with the impression it presents.

Since a brochure communicates both verbally and visually, it's a good idea to include lots of photos. These can be photos of you or your employees, your locations or your facilities, or of satisfied customers. Be sure and include photos of your product in use or finished projects you have completed for other customers. The more photos the better.

The cover of the brochure should include a headline that draws the prospect in. Ideally, this headline identifies who you are and what your company does, even before the brochure is opened. If the headline lends itself to repetition, try including it on each inside panel to reinforce its effectiveness. Whenever possible, include an interesting or entertaining photo on the brochure cover. The cover page has one definite purpose: It should proclaim READ ME!

Include
your logo
and tag
line in a
prominent
position.

If you're planning to mail your brochure, remember to leave room for the address. Most two-fold brochures use the center panel for mailing information.

The back page of your brochure is a good place to include a coupon or other free offer. Having read your brochure, invite the prospect to take some action. Encourage them to fill out a customer questionnaire, call your toll-free number, or use the convenient order form.

If it's at all economically feasible, print the brochure in color. Studies have shown that color increases retention rate by 57 percent and raises the inclination to buy by 41 percent!

Creating a brochure mock-up

Even if you decide to have your brochure designed and printed by professionals, it's helpful to make a mock-up in PhotoDeluxe Business Edition. This lets you take the time you need to play with text and photos, until you've got exactly the right "look and feel." When you're ready to produce the brochure, you can take your files to a service bureau. They'll use your mock-up as a guide and help you decide on paper and inks. The bureau can then do the ac-

To add interest to this text-heavy financial brochure, the photos were enhanced using the Special Effects > Elegant > Accent Edges guided activity

tual scanning, layout, and printing.

Many small-business brochures contain six panels with three panels on each side. Starting with a standard 8 1/2 x 11 piece of paper and folding it twice makes a six-panel brochure that is the ideal size for a standard #10 envelope. If you require a larger brochure, think in terms of fours (that is, four, eight, or twelve pages). Printing in multiples of four cuts down on printing costs.

When creating your mock-up, keep in mind the style and colors you've chosen for your business cards and stationery. You want the brochure to be part of a unified marketing package. Use the same font family that's on your other marketing materials and include your logo and tag line in a prominent position. If you've used PhotoDeluxe Business Edition templates for your cards and stationery, you may want to include some of the template artwork in your brochure.

Use the same font styles that are on your other marketing materials.

This brochure details information on both services and products

Printing it yourself

If you decide to print your brochure on your own color printer, you can create a very professional looking brochure using one of the many pre-folded, patterned papers available from mail-order companies. If you ask, most of these companies will send you a complete paper sampler for free. Try ordering in small quantities until you find a paper that you like and one that goes well with your template style and color. Order in bulk when you're ready to make a large print run.

Distributing your brochures

Brochures should not spread far and wide. Instead, distribute brochures selectively either to those who have specifically requested them or to carefully targeted prospects. Unless your product is very expensive, don't provide brochures to shoppers as this gives them an excuse not to buy. Instead, include a brochure with each purchase to encourage repeat business or word-of-mouth advertising.

When possible, personalize the brochure before you mail it. You might highlight information that you think might be of particular importance to the prospect or you can add handwritten notes in the margins. You can even use Post-its to draw attention to specific information.

When you're making an initial contact with a prospect, brochures are an excellent way to amplify a cold sales call or an introductory letter. As a follow-up, you can send a more complete folder of information (including press clippings, reprints from journals, or samples). Remember, the brochure is the lead in—it's up to you to make the sale. ■

Create a brochure cover from your business card

You can reuse elements from your business card to give your brochure the same look and feel as your card.

Open your business card in PhotoDeluxe and save it with a new name. Choose Merge Layers from the Layers palette.

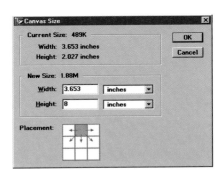

Click Advanced > Size > Canvas Size and increase the height to 8 inches. Click the top-center position in the placement box.

Choose a selection tool from the Selections palette to move the elements. To select and drag text, use the Object Selection tool. To select and drag artwork, use one of the shape tools or the Color Wand tool.

Newsletters

Communicating with customers

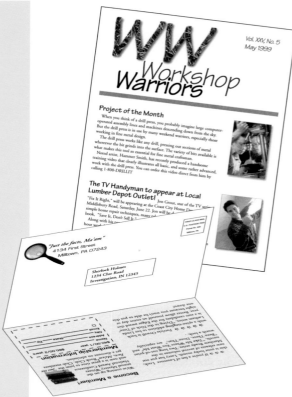

To a guerilla marketer, the phrase, "Oh, I forgot about you," are fighting words. Whether a customer is browsing or is ready to buy, your mission is to make sure that your name is the first one that comes to mind. A monthly or quarterly newsletter is one effective and entertaining way to remind people of who you are, what you do, and how much they need you.

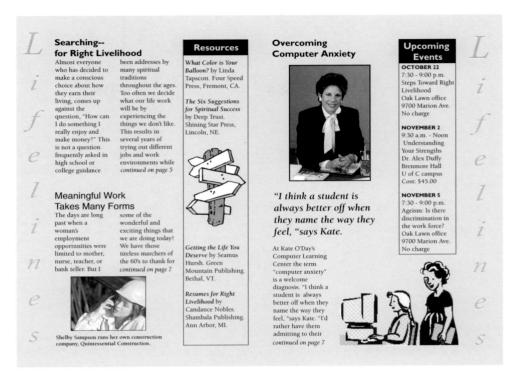

Searching--
for Right Livelihood

Almost everyone who has decided to make a conscious choice about how they earn their living, comes up against the question, "How can I do something I really enjoy and make money?" This is not a question frequently asked in high school or college guidance

been addresses by many spiritual traditions throughout the ages. Too often we decide what our life work will be by experiencing the things we don't like. This results in several years of trying out different jobs and work environments while continued on page 5

Meaningful Work
Takes Many Forms

The days are long past when a woman's employment opportunities were limited to mother, nurse, teacher, or bank teller. But I

some of the wonderful and exciting things that we are doing today! We have those tireless marchers of the 60's to thank for continued on page 7

Shelby Sampson runs her own construction company, Quintessential Construction.

Resources

What Color is Your Balloon? by Linda Tapscott. Four Speed Press, Fremont, CA.

The Six Suggestions for Spiritual Success by Deep Trust. Shining Star Press, Lincoln, NE.

Getting the Life You Deserve by Seamus Hursh. Green Mountain Publishing. Bethal, VT.

Resumes for Right Livelihood by Candance Nobles. Shambala Publishing. Ann Arbor, MI.

Overcoming
Computer Anxiety

"I think a student is always better off when they name the way they feel, "says Kate.

At Kate O'Day's Computer Learning Center the term "computer anxiety" is a welcome diagnosis. "I think a student is always better off when they name the way they feel, "says Kate. "I'd rather have them admitting to their continued on page 7

Upcoming
Events

OCTOBER 22
7:30 - 9:00 p.m.
Steps Toward Right Livelihood
Oak Lawn office
9700 Marion Ave.
No charge

NOVEMBER 2
9:30 a.m. - Noon
Understanding Your Strengths
Dr. Alex Duffy
Brenmore Hall
U of C campus
Cost: $45.00

NOVEMBER 5
7:30 - 9:00 p.m.
Ageism: Is there discrimination in the work force?
Oak Lawn office
9700 Marion Ave.
No charge

Newsletters are effective when you target the decision makers, that is, the people who make the actual purchases. This might be the consumer, a purchasing agent or department, or another small-business owner. Publishing a newsletter is a powerful way to build credibility and reinforce repetition and familiarity, those substantial cornerstones that build trust and confidence in your business. While many readers may only glance at the first page, they become more aware of your product. It's sort of the print equivalent of "Oh, I've heard so much about you."

Newsletters are entertaining when they communicate with your clients and prospects in a casual and relaxed way. Unlike advertising or direct mail, a newsletter can take the time to deliver a provocative mix of sales pitch, news, education, ideas, promotions, interviews, and even jokes and cartoons. By including useful and timely information, you turn the newsletter into a valuable resource, one that gains the respect and loyalty of your customers. For example, it you run a catering business, you might include favorite recipes, foods that are

Using black ink on colored paper is an inexpensive way to produce a two-color newsletter. The multiple columns, vertical type, and mixture of clip art and photos make this an eye-catching spread.

Newslet-
ters are
effective
when you
target the
decision
makers.

Newsletters

50

in season, what's new in party foods, or a profile of a recent, big-name client. If you're in real estate, you could include profiles of neighborhoods, the latest in building trends, information on mortgage rates, or articles on fixing up older homes.

Creating a lively design

Unless you're familiar with a page-layout program, such as Adobe PageMaker, you might want a professional to create your newsletter masthead and give you some advice on layout. But once you have the basic look, you can use PhotoDeluxe Business Edition to try out different combinations of copy and art.

Vol. XXV, No. 5
May 1999

Project of the Month

When you think of a drill press, you probably imagine large computer-operated assembly lines and machines descending down from the sky. But the drill press is in use by many weekend warriors, especially those working in fine metal design.

The drill press works like any drill, pressing out sections of metal whereever the bit grinds into the surface. The variety of bits available is what makes this tool so essential for fine metal craftsman.

Noted artist, Hammer Smith, has recently produced a handsome training video that clearly illustrates all basic, and some rather advanced, work with the drill press. You can order this video direct from him by calling 1-800-DRILLIT

The TV Handyman to appear at Local Lumber Depot Outlet!

Jon Grout, star of the TV series "Fix It Right," will be appearing at the Coast City Home Depot on Middlebury Road, Saturday, June 22. Jon will be demonstrating several simple home repair techniques, many taken from his newly published book, "Save It, Don't Sell It."

Along with his partner, Cindy Tiles, Jon will also conduct two three-hour workshops on Bathroom Design and Restoration. The workshops will be held in the Lumber Selection Room from 9am to noon, and 1pm to 4pm. Advance registration is recommended. Call 1-888-HOME for more information.

Drop shadows give photos more depth. These drop shadows were created using the Special Effects > Artistic > Drop Shadow guided activity

Creating a masthead

The masthead is the identifying information that appears across the top of the front page of your newsletter (it can also be repeated in whole or in part on the other pages). The masthead should include your company name and your logo, if you have one. You can also give your newsletter a whimsical or self-explanatory name. The object is to gain the reader's attention and establish your identity, all in the few seconds it takes someone to glance at the piece.

Keeping down costs

One way to keep down your newsletter costs is to design a color masthead and then have a large quantity printed. When publication time rolls around, print your black-and-white copy on the masthead. You'll end up with a professional-looking newsletter for a fraction of the cost of a full-color piece.

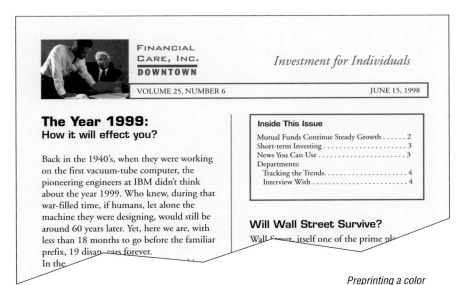

Preprinting a color masthead (and the rules) and then printing the content in black gives a professional look while significantly reducing costs

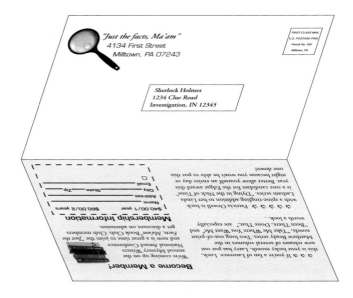

This self-mailer newsletter has the fold on the bottom and is sealed on the top using a sticker or a staple. Pieces that fold on the top need two fasteners and require special handling, increasing the mailing costs.

MARKETING TIPS

◆ Make your newsletter a combination of news, ideas, tips, and sales pitch

◆ Have a tone and focus

◆ Remember that customers love to see their name in print

◆ Make it easy to contact you

◆ Publish on a regular schedule

◆ Design the newsletter as a self-mailer to lower postage costs

Think of PhotoDeluxe as your creative white board. Try mixing and matching copy and art, or even seeing how the page might look printed on different paper. The trick with a newsletter is to make sure that related items stay together, and that the page doesn't look overwhelmed with either too much copy or too many headlines, boxes, dividers, or font styles.

If you have fewer, but longer items, use a few wide columns. Justify the text and then use rules to define the space. Or let the sharp edges of the white space divide up the copy. On the other hand, if you're including lots of little nuggets, use multiple columns so that you have more flexibility in how you lay out the page. Above all, keep the page inviting and clean—most readers think of newsletters as something to be read quickly.

Filling up the pages

The thought of being faced with four, or six, or eight empty pages once every quarter (or even worse, once every month), may paralyze you with fear.

What are you going to use to fill all those columns? One good idea is to have specific goals for your newsletter such as:

- I want investors to be able to make informed decisions.

- I want my customers to know that I take their needs seriously.

- I want to present my company as the leader in our field.

Then, keep those goals in mind as you develop a focus. Stick with the focus and both you and your readers will be less confused.

If you're still immobilized, you can hire a freelance writer. (Make sure, however, that you have the budget for outside help.) If it appears that it's up to you, take a few deep breaths and slowly ideas will emerge.

10 rules for effective newsletters

1. Include an interesting variety of news, education, resources, useful facts, and entertaining stories. A newsletter needs to be more than advertising and self-promotion.

2. Provide valuable, timely information. If it's out-of-date or boring, it's counterproductive.

3. Keep things short. Newsletters are popular because they don't take long to read.

4. Highlight your customers. Keep the tone friendly and personal.

5. Be sure your newsletter is easy to read and easy to look at.

6. Include ideas that enhance your reputation as an expert and important resource.

7. Publish on a regular schedule.

8. Send only to proven customers or hot prospects. Don't send it to people who never respond to your offers.

9. Make it easy to contact you by including addresses, toll-free numbers, and Web site information.

10. Motivate your readers to buy. A newsletter is a selling tool and people want to buy solutions to their problems.

Tasteful Catering

Vol.12, No.8

Serving clients in San Catherine county since 1974

WHERE DO I BUY...

The Best in Local Produce Summertime, and the meals are easy. With so much fresh fruit and produce at the markets, it's a snap to prepare healthy, tasty meals and snacks

Living in this wonderful county, we are fortunate indeed to have many sources for the fruits and vegetables so necessary in our daily diet. But keep in mind that much of this produce is not locally grown but is shipped in from other growing regions. Now, more than

ever, is the time to buy from local growers.

Pick Your Own We are coming into harvest seasons, and many local farmers are readying their annual pick you own seasons. By driving just a bit north, you can find strawberries, apricots,

THE HISTORY OF HERBS

Stalking the Wild Thyme Say the word "thyme" and one certain group of people immediately think of Simon and Garfunkel. Others, especially those from an island off the coast of Britain think of the bloomin' heather. But in
Con't on page 2

OUR CLIENTS DECIDE...
WHERE'S THE BEST PIZZA.

Pizza used to be a staple of the catering trade. A few years ago gourmet pizzas, a la Wolfgang Puck, were all the rage. But like Thai food before it, pizza is no longer served at most functions. Instead, it has reverted back to the perennial family and Friday-night date meal that it's been for decades.
Pizza lovers are a fanatical and loyal lot. If

you know anyone from Chicago, they will testify with their dying breath that there has never been a good pizza outside of the North Side. Gotta have the crust right, they sigh. And who ever heard of pineapple on a pizza??!! New Yorkers on the other hand, can be just as adamant that pizza never had so good before it was reinvented

PARTY PLANNING...
FAMOUS HOST, BELVA BEATRICE TELLS YOU HOW TO PLAN A FLAWLESS EVENT.

On a warm, sunny afternoon last week, we had the pleasure of meeting Belva Beatrice, host of TV's "PartyTime". Belva was in town to give a series of seminars on creating unique children's gatherings, including entertaining those hard to please pre-teen partygoers.
"Just as with any group, you have to keep in mind what the kids like

and what they hope to get our of their party," she said with a straight face. Being the mother of two twelve girls, we had to laugh. "I mean after getting the right boys to come," she smiled.
She stressed that kids want to have easy and fun food, but not something too unusual.

DESIGN TIPS

◆ Make the design fun and eye-catching

◆ Use boxes with shadows to set off information

◆ Create columns with rules or text justification

◆ Include a volume number or date

◆ Don't run headings across the entire column width

Here're a few topics that are proven newsletter draws:

- news of yourself and your industry

- a question-and-answer column

- tips and tricks

- profiles of employees or community leaders

- case histories

- company success stories

- reviews and write-ups of conferences

- reprints of articles of interest from trade publications (with permission)

- interviews with customers

- related news of interest from your field

There are also outside resources, whose business it is to provide filler, articles, and cartoons. Two of the most helpful are Pages Filler Service, put out by Berry Publishing of Chicago, Ill., and Newsletter Resources of St. Louis, Mo.

Who and how often?

The audience for your newsletter is partially defined by your business and partially defined by your focus and intent. In addition to current customers and prospects, consider sending the newsletter to the local Chamber of Commerce and to association lists. Leave the newsletter at locations that are likely to attract potential buyers. And don't overlook the business trade journals in your field—you might get some free publicity if you're referenced or quoted.

How frequently you distribute your newsletter is up to you. You can make it a quarterly, bimonthly, or even monthly publication. Or, you may want to limit it to Christmas and other heavy sales times. For your customers' convenience, include a volume number or date on each issue.

Whatever schedule you decide on, establish a routine and stick to it. You want to become habit-forming to your readers. ∎

Fix photos for printing

PhotoDeluxe Business Edition makes it easy to fix photos so that they will print better. This photo was prepared for print by increasing the contrast and simplifying the background.

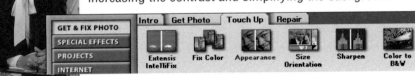

Choose Get & Fix Photo > Touch Up > Appearance to change contrast

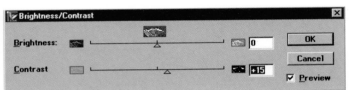

Using the slider in the dialog box, the contrast was increased to +15

To delete the old background, the woman was selected with the Smart Selection tool. The Invert button in the Selection palette was used to change the selection to the background. The background was then deleted using the Advanced > Edit > Delete tool.

The solid background color was added using the Advanced > Tools > Color Change tool

Web sites

Taking your identity online

B eing a guerrilla marketer, you know the importance of adapting to changing marketing circumstances. Well, no single marketing tool is growing and changing faster than the amazing, wonderful, World Wide Web. In the last few years, Web sites have sprouted up all over and no self-respecting small business would dream of being without one.

Choose Projects > Web > Banners to see the PhotoDeluxe Business Edition banner templates. You can choose from either vertical or horizontal banners. These two sites were developed from templates webanv22 and webanh21.

Small images equal faster download times and happier customers

Time to jump in

Because the Web is a new technology, you may be intimidated by the task of creating a Web site. But if you think about it, you already know a lot about designing for and marketing on the Web. The Web is part print (like your printed advertisements), part graphics (like your brochure and flyers), and mostly identity (which you have already established with your logo, business cards, and stationery). The great advantages of Web sites are that they are relatively cheap, they allow you to distribute a lot of information to a large audience, and they can be changed easily. Best of all, Web pages let you offer online buying. For more on this subject, see Web Advertising.

PhotoDeluxe Business Edition is an invaluable tool in helping you create and edit the photographs, banners, buttons, backgrounds, and titles that you'll include on your Web pages. When you're ready to put the Web site together, use a Web page-authoring application such as Adobe PageMill. In fact, you can copy your PhotoDeluxe Business Edition art directly to your Web page by choosing Send & Save > To Application > PageMill.

Web terminology

Like any other tribe, Websters have their own unique language. Once you learn a few basic terms, it's not difficult to converse in this foreign (and sometimes puzzlingly familiar) tongue. Here's your course on Webtalk 101:

- **Web page**—a page of coded text that tell a browser how to display it. In addition to text, Web pages can also contain pictures, sounds, tables, buttons, and animations.
- **site (or Website)**—a collection of related Web pages.
- **browser**—software that lets you look at Web sites. Two of the best-known browsers are Netscape Navigator and Microsoft Internet Explorer.
- **buttons**— text or graphics that are used as links.
- **links**—locations on a Web page that, when clicked, move you to a different place on the page or to an entirely different page.
- **download**—transfer the Web page contents from the Web to your computer so you can view it.
- **URL**—your site address, for example, http://www.pet sitters.com. To get to your site, users type the URL into their browser.

What's the point?

Before you do anything else, you need to decide on the purpose of the Web site. Will it be for information or will it include ordering capabilities? Do you want your customers to learn about your products or be amused and entertained? What action do you want customers to take after viewing the site? Do you want to refer them to other sites that complement your business? Once you know your site's purpose, designing it becomes much easier.

Designing the site

Many of the same marketing and design tips that apply to other forms of marketing also apply to Web pages; however, there are some differences. First of all, Web sites aren't linear. This means that readers click on links to jump around from page to page. Clicking links is fun, but can quickly deteriorate into confusion if you don't provide a foolproof way to get around (or navigate) the site.

This banner template (webanh26) uses only one font, making it easy to read. The colors define the navigation buttons.

DESIGN TIPS

◆ Provide banners for easy navigation

◆ Use a sans serif font for online text

◆ Make the text large enough to be read easily

◆ Limit the number of fonts and colors

◆ Test all links

Banners that repeat on every page make navigation as simple and apparent as possible. You'll win the gratitude of your customers if you make it easy to get to anywhere on the site (and then back again). In a banner, each graphic or word represents a particular page or section of the site. One click and you're there. Repeating the icon on the page you land on reinforces the link. PhotoDeluxe Business Edition provides both horizontal and vertical banners. To create Web banners and buttons, choose Projects > Web, then choose either the Banners, Buttons, or Titles guided activity.

Web page readers will be viewing your site in a variety of sizes (depending on their browsers and monitor sizes). Since people want to see less on a Web page than on a printed page, keep the information simple and short. To accommodate all your readers, make the first page fit within the standard 640 x 460 rectangle (the standard window size for browsers). Design all the pages so that they're no wider than 640 pixels. If readers must scroll, make them scroll down but never sideways.

Before

After

This background was created by choosing Get & Fix Photo > Get Photo > Sample Photos and then opening the rdleaves photo from the Web gallery. Using the Projects > Web > Background guided activity, the contrast was lowered and the image transparency was set to 30%. As a final touch, the Special Effects > Cool > Chalk & Charcoal guided activity was used to apply a light green color.

Text size on the Web page is tricky, since you can't set the size that will appear on the screen (the reader's browser does that). When you want to control the size of text, turn it into a graphic. You can define the dimensions of graphics so that they're the same size in every browser.

Using color

One of the great things about Web pages is that they're in color and the color doesn't cost anything extra! By picking a few colors and mixing and matching them wisely, you can create a "palette" for your site.

The background of your Web pages has the largest influence on your color scheme. PhotoDeluxe Business Edition offers you lots of choices for backgrounds, from simple, subtle colors to intricate patterns. When you're creating a background, be sure it complements your other art and is light enough for the text to be read easily. To create a background for your site, choose Projects > Web > Backgrounds.

The background shown on the previous page as it appears on a page in the PageMill Web page-authoring application (the page was developed using the webanh41 template). The dark text provides a good contrast against the light background and the text size is large enough to be read easily.

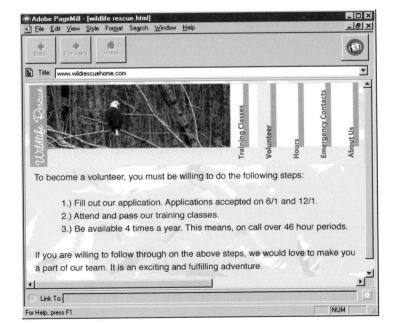

Make sure the title of your home or entry page is clear and descrip- tive.

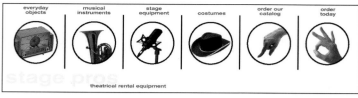

Using the same banner at the top of every page makes navigation simple. This banner was created using the webanh25 template.

Including photos

Using photos and other graphics is a very important element in designing a creative and interesting site. Keep your images small. Larger images take longer to download and will try the patience of even your most loyal customer. Choose Get & Fix Photo > Clip Art > Webart to see the PhotoDeluxe Business Edition graphics especially designed for the Web.

Preparing the photo for the Web is simple using PhotoDeluxe Business Edition. You don't need to study resolution or file formats, and you don't need to know about color bits and anti-aliasing. When you're ready to go, simply choose Send & Save > Email/Web > Web page. Follow the guided activity and your photo will be saved in the right resolution and format using browser-safe colors.

Register your site

Now that you've created your simple, compelling, informative, and entertaining Web site, you need to let others know about it. After all, if you want your Web site to help you generate more profits, you need to bring it to the attention of potential customers and clients.

You've probably used some of the search engines and directories on the Web (such as Yahoo, Lycos, Alta Vista, or InfoSeek) to find information. Well, you can use these same search sites to publicize your own site. Look on the service's main page and you'll see a small button that says "Add your site," "Submit your URL," or "Get Listed." Don't be alarmed if you send off your site name and it doesn't immediately appear in the listings. It takes anywhere from a few days to several weeks for the registration to take effect.

Instead of registering your site on each search engine individually, you can use a submission service. These services post your URL in several engines simultaneously. Two popular submission services are Submit It! at *www.submit-it.com* and Register-it! at *www.register-it.com.*

Some search services go through Web sites periodically looking for sites to add to their databases. Sometimes humans do this; other sites use automated "robots" or "spiders" to do the search. Here're two ways to increase the chances that your site will be chosen for the database and that it will draw customers:

- Make sure the title of your home or entry page is clear and descriptive. Many services use the page title as a deciding criterion for listing the site.

- Use an opening paragraph on your entry page that tells the reader what to expect on the site. Often search engines include part of the first paragraph in the site description.

Banners can be customized to include your logo and tag line. The webanh26 template was modified to create this banner.

◆ Keep your site unique and up-to-date

◆ Include online ordering forms

◆ Register your site

◆ Cross-market by including your URL on cards, letterhead, and brochures

◆ Advertise on other sites or barter with another site for additional exposure

Keep it current

Getting your site up and running is a major achievement. Sites, however, are not static entities. You need to keep your site up-to-date, changing the information periodically to keep your customers coming back. Also, be sure and check the outside links on your site frequently. If another site changes its name or no longer exists, your link will be dead. Nothing is less professional or

Create a patterned background

To create an eye-catching background, the Special Effects > Collage > Pattern Fill guided activity was used on part of a photo

In the Pattern step, the dollar sign was selected using the Rectangle selection tool

In the Fill step, the opacity was lowered in the Selection Fill dialog box

more frustrating than the dreaded "File not found" error message.

If your site changes a lot in content, for example, if you publish an online newsletter, consider keeping an archive of back issues. To quickly direct customers to changed content, include a "What's New" page with a prominent link on the first page. You can also clue in customers to changed content by including a revision date on the first page. ■

After completing the Pattern Fill guided activity, the Advanced > Effects > Special Effects > Blur > Circular guided activity was applied to the patterned photo

Getting Into Print

Magazines

Going for maximum exposure

As a small-business owner, your first response to the topic of magazine advertising is probably "Forget it!" Who has the budget for magazine advertisements? But before you dismiss the idea completely, put on your guerrilla uniform and take another look. There is a time and a place for magazine advertising. It just requires a little imagination and investigation.

Parlez-vous vacation?

Now is the time and we have the fare!

Your avon leaves from
Metropolian Airport
3 times a day.
Bon Voyage!

Way Out Travel
Call: 1-800-555-UFLY

This travel ad grabs attention with its great photograph and intriguing headline

Selecting the magazines

Let's face it—there's nothing better for your prestige than running a full-page advertisement in one of the high-circulation, mass-distribution, consumer-oriented magazines. But is this good guerrilla strategy? How many real prospects will you reach in such a large and mixed readership? What fairy godfather is financing this endeavor? Well, before you give up your burning desire to appear in *Time*, there is a compromise solution. Advertise your product in a regional edition of a national magazine.

Regional editions include special inserts full of local advertisements. You can find out which magazines have regional issues by checking the Consumer Magazine and Agri-Media Rate and Data (published by Standard Rate and Data Service, Inc., also known as SRDS). You'll find this helpful publication in the library. You can also find out the advertising rates for these regional issues. For an even better deal in a regional edition, you can purchase remnant space from the publisher or an agency.

Galleria Sophia

Contemporary Italian Art

Diana Mezzetti

Uno Fiore   48" x 60"   Oil

Fuller at Fulton, New York, NY 12345
800-ITALIAN   www.bueno.com

*The sophisticated tone
of this ad would go well
in* The New Yorker

After you've figured out what regional edition to use, **run the ad once.** Then, sit back and capitalize on the publicity forever! Get a million reprints of the ad and stick on a label that reads "As seen in *People* magazine" or "Featured in the latest edition of *Sports Illustrated*." Some guerrilla marketers have used these reprints for years!

Another effective way to use magazines is to run an ad in a specialty or trade magazine that hits your target market straight on. To find out what magazines are available, check Business Publication Rates and Data (another publication of SRDS). After you've gotten some names, send away for sample copies. When you find likely candidates, run your ad consistently in these smaller magazines to build up customer familiarity and confidence.

Doing the two-step

(Step One) Run a magazine display ad that hits the high points of your offering. Then tell readers to call or write for free information.

(Step Two) When they respond, send them your brochure and a motivating sales letter.

Bright colors, a familiar headline, and good use of white space draws parents into this ad—perfect for a family magazine

Research shows...

- Two-page spreads attract 25% more readers than one-page ads
- A half-page ad is about two-thirds as effective as a full-page ad
- Full-color pages attract about 40% more readers than black-and-white pages
- Position in the front or back of the magazine does not matter
- Readership does not drop off when an ad is run several times
- Photographs are more effective than drawings
- Illustrations showing the product in use are more effective than static illustrations
- Ads with people in them have a higher response rate

Match the ad to the magazine

Newspaper readers want the facts, and they want them fast. You only have a millisecond to grab their attention. Magazine readers are a different breed. They are purchasing a more sophisticated form of entertainment, one presented in full-color, glossy pages. They generally read their magazines over a period of time; this means your magazine ad has a

Visit a Tropical Paradise, Every Day
PISCES AQUARIUMS
Your aquarium experts for 25 years.

Enjoy the beauty and tranquility of rare and exotic marine life in your own home.

1-800-555-4355
300 Beau Way, Seaton, IA 12345
Free delivery and setup of all aquariums

Adding a wave shape to this ad visually reinforces the company's positioning

72

longer shelf life than a newspaper ad. It also means the ad can contain more information. You already have the reader's attention. Your job is to motivate them to buy.

Magazine readers expect a certain tone and quality from this more expensive medium. Your ad will bring better results if it matches the magazine's editorial approach. For example, the tone may be dignified (*The New Yorker*), timely and trustworthy (*Newsweek*), traditional and home-oriented (*Family Circle*), or irreverent, hip, and chaotic (*Wired*). Whatever the magazine's outlook, make sure your ad fits its style.

Magazines come with predefined audiences. This means you can write the ad with the assurance that each reader is a potential prospect. Speciality magazines, such as *Business Week, Motor Trend, Sports Illustrated, Popular Photography, Better Homes and Gardens, BabyTalk, Scientific American,* and *Food and Wine,* have a hard-earned reputation for knowledge and expertise. Advertising in these magazines carries the reader's trust and confidence over to your product. (You can view the online version of *Business Week* directly from PhotoDeluxe

The Perfect Moment

All it takes is a little planning.

Wonderful Weddings
Wedding Planners • Full service
1•100•YOURDAY
774 First Ave., Riverside, IN 12345

Business Edition. Just click Internet > Internet > Business Week.)

Designing the ad

Creating a brilliant magazine ad is a little trickier than writing a classified ad. For one thing, the competition is tougher. Magazine ads are classier, more creative, and often produced by high-priced ad agencies. Your ad needs to look at least as good as the surrounding ads. If you can afford to hire a graphic designer, do it. (If you can't afford it, try bartering.) Whether you're doing it yourself or working with a designer, it's a good idea to play around with the design in PhotoDeluxe Business Edition before you spend any money. To begin, ask yourself these questions:

- How big do I want the ad to be?

- How many photographs or illustrations do I want to include?

- Should it have a little or a lot of text?

Text-heavy ads project a more informational and scientific tone

Remnant space and per inquiry ads

Many magazines and newspapers have leftover space that is wasted if it's not filled with advertisements. Smart guerrillas take advantage of this remnant space to get their ads printed for half-price or less. One way to get a profitable deal for both you and the publisher is to run a full-page ad in the same spot every week. In return, ask the paper to run dozens of tiny remnant space fillers throughout the paper or magazine, referring to the big ad.

Small, specific-interest magazines are great for remnant space. Try presenting your ad in several different sizes. Tell the owner you'll pay some percentage of the rate card whenever your ad appears. This provides the publisher with a guaranteed cash flow and you with maximum exposure on a regular basis.

National magazines run regional editions that use 4-, 8-, or 16-page inserts to run local ads. If not all the pages are sold, they are stuck with empty space. If you get there at the right time, you can buy this space at a fantastic price, for example, $300 for a full-page, black-and-white ad in *Time*. Media Networks is a company that buys remnant space from national magazines and then sells it to small businesses.

Some magazine ads rely almost entirely on one large visual, with only small bits of text. If you opt for this design, make sure the words are explosive, intriguing, funny, motivating, or benefit-filled. Since magazines reproduce color very well, don't be timid with your colors. Make them attract the eye and jump off the page (as long as bold, vivid color is in keeping with the magazine's editorial mood and your own marketing identity). If the magazine or your product is more conservative, use subtle colors in an interesting way.

Other magazine ads are very text-heavy. This is fine since magazines readers tend to browse through their magazines and are known to read everything (including the advertisements). You've undoubtedly seen those magazine ads for weight-loss miracles and instant financial success. These ads typically show a very small photo of the owner or a satisfied customer and then continue with several columns of very small type (come on, admit that you've read at least one of these things). If the benefit or offer is what the customer is looking for (Re-

When you're testing out a new campaign or selling a product directly to the public, per inquiry ads can be a real money-saver. In a per inquiry ad, you pay nothing up front. The publication gets a share of all the sales you make as a result of the ad. If your ad works, you can end up paying more than you would have if you'd bought the space. When a per inquiry ad is successful, it's time to switch to remnant advertising. If your ad is a bust, nobody makes any money. The two advantages of per inquiry ads are that you get a free trial run for your ad and you get to run an ad that you otherwise might not have been able to afford.

MARKETING TIPS

◆ Match the tone and quality of the ad to the magazine

◆ Use really great photography

◆ Buy space in a regional edition

◆ Run an expensive ad once and use the reprints forever

◆ Run A/B splits to test magazine ads

◆ Consider placing ads in appropriate trade journals

Testing with A/B splits

Testing your magazine advertising is made easier thanks to the availability of A/B splits. You send the publication two different ads, varying your headline or offer. The first ad is run in the first half of the magazine run (A) and the second ad in the second half of the run (B). You get to test two ads for the price of one. Be sure and code the addresses or phone numbers so that you can track the responses from each ad.

grow Your Hair Naturally!), they'll be patient enough to read through the entire thing. This type of magazine ad is fine, as long as it fits the magazine tone and is appropriate to your product. As the owner or distributer of the product, you're in the best position to know what will attract your customers.

There aren't any templates for advertisements in PhotoDeluxe Business Edition, but it's easy to make your own. First decide how big the ad will be. Unless you're placing a classified-type ad in the back of *Rolling Stone* or *PC World*, your ad needs to be big. The bigger the better. Take a minute now and look at some magazine ads. You'll notice that most of them fill the page.

Asking the customer to bring in the ad for a free offer lets you compare the relative effectiveness of two different headlines

Once you have a general idea of the size, create a PhotoDeluxe Business Edition file. Add some photos and enter some text. It doesn't have to be the actual pictures or make any grammatical sense. Try fooling around with colors, sizes, and effects. Gradually, your ad will take shape and you'll be ready to work on the real, final design.

Make the most of your investment

One of the most valuable side effects of magazine advertising is the merchandising aids offered by most publications. For little or no additional cost, you can get a variety of useful items such as easel-back cards, reprints, decals, and mailing folders. The uses for the reprints alone are endless and invaluable: as signs in your window, as enclosures in direct mailings, as additions to proposal letters, as advertisement on bulletin boards, as counter cards, as display pieces at trade shows, or as part of a brochure or circular. Magazine ads are truly the one-time investment that keeps on giving! ■

Try out different designs

After checking their budget, this company decided to place a medium-sized ad. A photograph was selected and the copy was written. While this was an acceptable ad, there wasn't anything that really made the ad stand out.

Using layers to keep the elements separate, the designer experimented with several different combinations of art and text.

After cutting down on text, enlarging the photograph, and adding a wavy shape, this ad jumps off the page. Color was added to highlight the key points, such as free delivery. Adjusting the alignment divided the text into easy-to-read blocks.

"I had the wedding of my dreams...."
And so can you.

Wonderful Wed
Wedding Planners • Ful
1•100•YOURL
774 First Ave., Riverside, I

This Weekend Only
ALL AQUATIC PLANTS
35% to 50% OFF!

EXOTIC
FLORAL
DESIGNS

SALE AT BOTH STORES
7418 Highway 36, Mantoon and
322 High St, Dundee

SPECIAL HOURS 8 AM to 8 PM
1-800-555-2334

Newspapers
Spreading the good news

Even with phenomenal growth of the Web, newspaper display ads are still the most popular advertising medium for small businesses. Newspaper ads are inexpensive and allow you to reach a large number of people in a targeted geographical area. People enjoy browsing through newspaper ads because they can take their time absorbing the information. Online viewing has not yet reached that level of leisurely pursuit for most of us.

Using one large photograph and minimal copy allows this ad to be changed easily yet still evoke a sense of familiarity

Capture Today....
For All Your Tomorrows.

Groups

Formal

Informal

Jan Jordon • Child Photography
1•800•555•2212

Almost everyone likes to newspaper-shop before they go out to make a purchase. Your job is to make sure that their eyes stop at your ad, they read your copy, they are motivated to buy, and they remember your company or product. You've got lots of competition in newspaper advertising, not just from the news, and not just from others in your business, but from all the department stores, furniture showrooms, car dealerships, sports outlets, and travel companies that are vying for the consumer's attention and dollars.

Where should you run your ad?

Probably the first place you think of to run your ad is in the newspaper you read. This may or may not be the best place to advertise. You need to ask your-self what paper does your target audience read? Within that paper, is there a specific section that would be better than others? For example, if you're advertising a food item or service, you'd want to appear on the day the food section appears, preferably in the food section. If you're trying to reach sports enthusiasts, your best bet is to advertise in the sports section on Mondays. If you're aiming at business people, run your ad in the business section.

What
newspaper
does your
target
audience
read?

You'll get the most readers if you advertise in the general news section. If you're going for the general reader, be extremely insistent that your ad appear in the front section on a right-hand page, above the fold. Placing a large volume of ads is always helpful when you're trying to negotiate a prime location.

Don't limit yourself to metropolitan newspapers. Once you go looking, you'll be amazed at the number of newspapers that are around: local newspapers, national newspapers, daily newspapers, weekly newspapers, monthly newspapers, shopper-oriented newspapers, classified-ad newspapers, campus newspapers, and ethnic newspapers, to name just a few. And don't overlook the trade journals if your target market is likely to be reading them.

Always on Sunday

Your aim is to reach your prospect just at the moment that they're making a decision to go shopping. That's why it is so important to choose the right paper, the right section, and the right day. In most cases, you'll want to advertise on the days that you're open, but this is not always the case. The increased circulation of a Sunday issue, for example, might be a better alternative (even if you're not open on Sundays).

This headline imparts a sense of urgency. The background (created using the Special Effects > Bas Relief guided activity) is compelling even through it's not in color.

Offer a solution to a problem in the headline. Small areas of color can effectively highlight critical information.

What size can you can afford?

Before you do anything, call the newspaper and ask for a media kit that includes a rate card (advertising rates). This handy kit also contains information on production requirements, editorial policies, and audience analysis. Some media kits even contain an editorial calender that lists upcoming features. Depending on your product or service, you may want to time your advertising so that it appears with a feature designed to attract the largest concentration of your target audience.

The rate card lets you know how often you can advertise (good guerrillas always stays within their advertising budget). Most newspapers are 22 inches high and six columns wide and charge for advertising by the column inch. Suppose the newspaper charges a dollar a line (there are 14 lines per inch). To run a full-page ad, it would cost you 14 x 22 (for the inches) x 6 (for the columns) or $1848.00. If you make the add a bit smaller, however, say 12 inches high by four columns wide, the price drops dramatically to $672.00.

Is bigger always better?

Don't despair if you can't afford a big ad. Many studies have shown that consistency, repetition, and reinforcement are more important than size in newspaper advertising. For every three advertisements viewed, the average consumer ignores two. They need nine exposures to an ad before they remember it and up to 27 viewings before they feel familiar enough to buy the product. If you run your smaller ad over and over again, preferably in the same location, it will bring you much more business than a one-time run of a full-page ad.

Creating an effective ad

Don't underestimate the importance of your ad's appearance. Far more people will see your ad than will see you or your place of business. You want your ads to have a unique advertising identity that complements your marketing identity. Don't just plan one ad—envision the entire campaign. Give your ads a look and emotional tone that you can repeat over and over. For example, use an eye-catching headline that lends itself to variation or always invoke the same mood with your photographs. At the same time, be sure each ad contains an element of intrigue or surprise. An

"I had the wedding of my dreams...."
And so can you.

Wonderful Weddings
Wedding Planners • Full service
1•100•YOURDAY
774 First Ave., Riverside, IN 12345

easily recognizable ad increases consumer familiarity, and familiarity breeds success.

Above all, your ads should be informative. Talk to the readers in a personal way as you gently persuade them to read on. Start with what your readers know, then charm them with a story or build their desire with a promise. Remember, you need to make it very clear why your product is just what they need and have been waiting for.

Designing and writing the ad

There are three things that contribute to the ad's impact: the art, the copy, and the white space. All three need to be incorporated into a simple concept with a bold visual impact. Study a few newspaper ads and you'll see that the layout usually directs the eye to the upper left, sweeps across the page in an S-curve, and then comes to rest at the lower right. This classic design may work for you, but don't be afraid to break out of the mold.

Always include a great photograph or illustration in your ad. A picture truly is as effective as a thousand words (which would be a truly large ad!). Show your product in use, depict happy, satisfied customers, or feature your own smiling face. The photograph or illustration should be the visual focus.

Providing two slightly different addresses lets you track which ad produces a better response

6 BOOKS FOR ABSOLUTELY NOTHING!

(well, you do have to send in the coupon)

"Just the facts, Ma'am" Book Club gives you 6 FREE books, just for checking out our offer.

Yes, Send me your catalogs of the world's most exciting mysteries!

Name_____
Address_____
City_____
State_____
Phone_____

4134 First Street
Department A
Milltown, PA 07243
800-555-0187

YOU JUST CAN'T BEAT THIS OFFER!

(well, you do have to send in the coupon)

"Just the facts, Ma'am" Book Club gives you 6 FREE books, just for checking out our offer.

Yes, Send me your catalogs of the world's most exciting mysteries!

Name_____
Address_____
City_____
State_____
Phone_____

4134 First Street
Department B
Milltown, PA 07243
800-555-0187

The copy of the ad can vary from a few words to many paragraphs. If it's appropriate, don't shy away from long copy. People want to be informed and if you need to explain how something works or elaborate on benefits, go ahead. One of the things that consumers like about newspaper ads is that they can study them. So, if necessary, use lots of words.

The first and most important piece of copy is the headline. If you don't snag them with the headline, it doesn't matter what the rest of the ad says. In general, newspaper readers are scanning the ads with one question in mind, "What can this product do for me?" Answering this question with your headline is one sure way to get and keep their attention.

Make sure your headline includes at least one benefit. Use words like FREE, TIMESAVING, NEW, and SUCCESS. Tell the customer what they will get. For example, instead of saying "These are the world's best seeds," tout the results with "Have the world's most beautiful garden." Or use the headline to begin

Small ads are very successful when run regularly in the same place in the same publication. Clip art adds visual interest to this text-heavy ad.

Small ads

As a guerrilla, you know that you don't have to be big to be successful. Small display ads are often just as effective and profitable as large ones. A small ad is defined as one that is one column wide (about two inches) and from two to five inches tall. To make the most of your small ad, keep these tips in mind:

- Use a border or cross over a border to make your ad seem bigger.

- Like attracts like. Run your small add in a publication with a lot of others that are similar to it.

- Make your product obvious. Outline the benefit in your headline or use an attention-getting graphic.

- Stress how easy it is to get in touch with you by including an 800 number.

- Run the ad for a long, long time. Consistency and repetition are more important than size.

Small ads lend themselves well to running on a remnant basis. Their size makes them easy to fit into otherwise unusable spaces. If you negotiate a long contract that runs your add on a space-available basis, your small ad can reap big returns.

telling a story such as "The deck was half-finished when my sander broke again!" Your main goal is to establish the context and explain why "this ad is for you."

The body copy is where you have the most freedom. If you can't think of anything to say, start jotting down why you're creating the ad and what results you'd like to get. Think about the nice things your customers have said about your product or the questions they've asked. Persuasion is the key and you want to create a desire as you build interest. Always include a compelling offer that motivates the customer to take action. This might be a price, a coupon, a limited time frame, or the prominent display of an 800 number. Use short words and sentences to keep the copy easy to read.

Your closing copy should make the sale. End with a motivating tag line (Act now!) or reiterate what the customers will get from your product. Add your identification at the very bottom of the ad. You'll probably want to include

Don't stop running an ad until it doesn't work any- more.

your logo. Always make sure the customer knows how to find you by including your name, address, phone number, and hours.

Testing your ad

Since newspaper ads are relatively cheap, you can afford to run your ad in more than one newspaper. Don't be afraid that people will see your ad too many times. There is no such thing as too much exposure in newspaper advertising.

Running ads in several papers presents a great opportunity to test the ad's effectiveness. Try out two completely different ads, or vary one component, such as a headline. To gauge the response, tell the reader to bring in the ad, or question your customers as to how or where they heard about you. You can also include a coupon in each ad with a slightly different address. That way, you'll know that all responses sent to Department D came from the daily paper while those sent to Department S came from the shopper-oriented newspaper.

Put text over a photo

When you're using a template, the placement of the text is predetermined for you but you can add text anywhere in the photo by using the Text tool.

This photograph from the Samples Photo folder was converted to black and white using the Get & Fix Photo > Touch Up > Color to B & W guided activity

To make the text stand out, the photograph was lightened using the Special Effects > Transform > Make Transparent guided activity

Once the test results are in, run the most effective ad in the most productive newspaper, over and over and over again. Don't stop because you're sick of it or your family is sick of it or you can't stand to look at it one more time. The cardinal rule of newspaper advertising is: Don't stop running an ad until it doesn't work anymore! ■

The text was added using the Text tool

Classifieds

Making every word count

Y ou probably read the classifieds when you want to find a job, buy a car, or move to a new place. The next time you're browsing through the paper, however, take another look. Classifieds are the main form of advertising for many guerrilla enterprises, especially those that offer services. You can be pretty sure that if someone is bothering to read your classified ad, they're interested in buying. It's hard to resist an advertising medium with such pulling power.

When
you're
writing a
classified
ad, you
need to
make every
word
count.

Classifieds

89

Who could resist this headline?

GIVE YOUR KIDS A KICK!

Sign them up now for summer soccer camp. Group and individual workshops.
Call Today!
(123) 555-1211

Bernadette Keller
Sports Trainer

If you've about run out of advertising budget, classified ads are a dream come true. For very little outlay, you get flexibility, ready availability, free production, simple alteration, ease of testing, and great return—once you've honed the ad to perfection.

Writing the headline

When you're writing a classified ad, you need to make every word count. This doesn't mean that the ad needs to be short, but it does need to have punch. You want to catch the reader's eye, solve their problem, and make them call you.

A headline is essential and should be printed in capital letters. Make your headline appeal to the reader by asking a question (NEED AN ESTIMATE TODAY?), making an irresistible offer (ONLY $10 A MONTH!), or employing intrigue (PARADISE FOR THE ASKING). Then, let the rest of the ad expand on this theme. Use powerful words, such as fast, efficient, honest, reliable, and quality. End with the big guns: GUARANTEED, DISCOUNT, and FREE BROCHURE.

Display advertising in the classified section

Some newspapers and magazines run classified display ads. These are slightly larger ads that appear in the classified section but have a box around them. Classified display ads feature dark, large, display type and possibly even a graphic. They cost a bit more but are still considered classified ads. This extra touch might be just what your ad needs to get effective results.

Catering

| BIRTHDAYS OUR SPECIALITY **Kid's Catering 555-3344** | **Gourmet/Specialty Foods** Discover Delicious New Ideas in Food! *Gourmet Today* **555-1378** |

Elegant Catering For All Occasions
Tasteful Catering
- Theme Planning
- Weddings
- Dinner Parties
- Party Trays
- Buffets
- Bar-B-Q's

555-FOOD
"Make every event a Tasteful Event!"
123 Yummy Lane • Cherry Hill

CUSTOM DESIGNED PIES
for All Occassions
Call Meg at 555-9089

UNEXPECTED GUESTS TONIGHT?
Gourmet Express
Order by 3, Delivered by 6
1-888-DELIVER

Classified display ads cost a bit more but really shine in a sea of words. This ad, originally designed in color for the Yellow Pages, works equally well as a black-and-white classified display ad.

If you're stuck on how to begin writing the ad, look to that old adage, "imitation is the sincerest form of flattery." Find an ad that appeals to you and has been running for a long time, then mimic it. If it's been running a long time, it's probably working. This will get you started. After a bit of trial and error (the only error being that the ad didn't pull), you'll be ready to create an ad that dramatically distinguishes you from the competition.

Another technique is to think of the ad as your sales pitch. What do you say in the first few minutes when you're talking to a prospective customer? Get this message into your classified ad.

Making your ad stand out

Use short sentences and stick to the facts in the ad copy. Remember, these are prospects, not browsers. Avoid abbreviations or jargon unless you're sure that 99% of the readers will understand what you mean. One way to set your ad apart from the others is to use plain, speaking language instead of "want-ad talk." Phrase the ad so that it has a personal tone. For

EVER GREEN LAWN SERVICE

Complete lawn care. Installation, sod
lawns, design, and consulting.
License#330332

Call:(123) 555-1217

See our work at:
www.lawnservices.com

Moving this ad from the larger Gardening section to the smaller Landscaping section might increase response significantly

example, your ad might begin, "I LOVE MY JOB. When someone calls with a plumbing problem, I'm eager to help them—right away." Compare this with EXPERIENCED PLUMBER reliable, comparable rates, any problem. Which one would you call?

Too often, placers of classified ads forget to include vital information such as price, location, phone numbers, or hours. This can be fatal. On the other hand, you can use these omissions as a strategy. By leaving out something essential, you make the customer contact you. This strategy is a candidate for testing.

Using everything you've got

There's not a lot of design involved in a classified ad. Since you're dealing only with words, you're pretty much limited to small variations in typeface or size to make an impact. Use bold type, but sparingly, so that key points are immediately visible. Some newspapers also allow you to use reverse type (white type on a black background). This can be especially effective for a headline, company name, or phone number. If you have a logo, try to include it in the ad.

Where to place your classified ad

If your product or service requires customers in close physical proximity (and most retail businesses do), place your ad in the daily and weekly newspaper. You may choose to run the ad in the general classified section or in the business-to-business section. Depending on your product, your ad might also do well in a classified-only newspaper, such as the

Classified Flea Market or your local *Pennysaver*. Look over the categories and check out the competition to find out which newspaper is the right fit.

If your business appeals to a national audience, consider placing the ad in the classified section of an appropriate magazine. More and more magazines are coming to the conclusion that small businesses want to advertise nationally, but can't afford magazine display ad rates. Hence the growth of the classified sections of such publications as

*A thick border can help a
small ad seem larger*

The guerrilla gospel of classified ads

If you decide that classified ads are the best way for you to advertise, you should subscribe to the monthly newsletter put out by Agnes Franz of Agnes Franz Advertising. This publication is filled with advice on layout, classified ad use, where to advertise, how to design creative ads, and so on. Write to Classified Communications, P.O. Box 4242, Prescott, AZ 86302.

Rolling Stone, House and Garden, PC World, and that old standby, *The New Yorker*. Research has shown that your magazine classified ad has a very good chance of being read; 61% of Americans read magazines from the back to the front.

Getting a discount

Classified ads don't cost much to begin with and are made even cheaper when you take advantage of a frequency discount. For example, if you run a 5-line classified ad once, the cost might be $20. The same ad run three times would cost about $18 for each appearance, and only around $15 for five insertions. Since everyone doesn't read the classifieds every day (or every week or month for magazines), it makes sense to run your ad several times in the same category and same location before judging whether it's working or not.

You don't need to limit your ad to one category. Classified ads are a good way to test ads by running them in different categories. If you sell rare books, for ex-

BF Construction

Home Repair & Ugrades

Bill Ferry

General Contractor
123-555-1333
Lic# 123456123

Use reverse type to make your headline or company name more visible

ample, you might advertise in both the Books Sellers and Antiques sections. Or if you do computer consulting, you might place the ad in Business Services and Personal Computers.

If nothing else, classified ads are an inexpensive way to gain valuable information about the pulling power of specific products or claims, prices, head-lines, and various approaches to the copy. Use the classifieds as a testing ground and when you've gained experience and compared results, use this information in a display ad. This is not a foolproof method, however, since often classified ads get better results than display ads! ■

Add a border around your ad

Two of the best ways to make an ad stand out are to add a thick border and use reverse type.

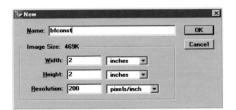

Create a new file for your classified ad

Click the All button in the Selections palette to choose the entire window

To add the border, click Advanced > Effects > Outline

In the Outline dialog box, enter a value for the border (about 15 pixels creates a wide border) and then choose black for the color

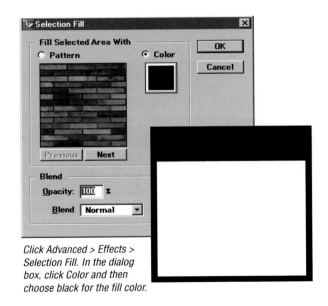

Click Advanced > Effects > Selection Fill. In the dialog box, click Color and then choose black for the fill color.

To make type stand out, try white type on a black background. Use the Rectangle tool to select the area that will contain the text.

Click the None button in the Selection palette to deselect the filled area, then use the Text tool to enter the headline text. Be sure to set the text color to white before closing the Text Tool dialog box.

Yellow Pages ads

Mining the hottest prospects

Think like a guerrilla. You don't have a lot of money for advertising. You're offered the chance to place an ad in a publication that goes to every household in your target market, free of charge. Only people who are ready to buy use this publication. Would you go for it? Think Yellow Pages.

Photos and maps make your Yellow Pages ads more personal and prompt more responses

Because of their high cost, the Yellow Pages are often underused by small-business owners. They have forgotten one of the basic guerrilla advertising tenets: The cost of advertising is not measured in dollars but in response!

For every owner who thinks the Yellow Pages are too expensive, there are several who swear it has been the entire reason for their success. It all depends on your product or service. And on how big of an ad you can afford.

If you're in retail, the Yellow Pages are probably a good bet. If you're an artist or consultant, however, a Yellow Pages ad may not be worth the cost. Take a look at the categories and see if your competition is advertising. If competitors are there, try and find out if it's paid off for them. Ponder whether your business lends itself to the language used in Yellow Page ads (mostly plucky adjectives).

Beating the competition

90% of the time that people reach for the Yellow Pages, they're looking for a vendor. This is the good news. The bad news is that when they find you, ALL your competition is listed there as well. Your mission is to make your ad the one that grabs and holds their interest.

The most obvious way to get attention is to be the biggest kid on the block. Or, at least bigger than most of the kids in your class. (The advertiser with the largest Yellow Pages ad gets called the most often by an alarmingly overwhelming number of customers.) Before you place your ad, do a little in-

The unusual cropping of the guitar photo provides an interesting border for this Yellow Pages ad

vestigation. Let your fingers walk through the category you'll be listed under. Who and what's already there? What can you do differently?

If you can't come up with a way to stand out, how about a smaller category? It often pays to be the biggest fish in a small pond. Try listing yourself under Dancing-Telegrams instead of Entertainers, or bypass the crowded Travel Agencies category for the Cruises listings.

If you haven't started your business yet and don't have the budget to be big, at least you can be first. Name your company something that will appear as the first entry in a category, for example,

Abacus Art Supplies, Abatement Pest Control, or Apricot Computer.

Packing in the information

As you begin writing your Yellow Pages ad, think about the questions that a person looking in that section would ask. The answer to "Where will I have the largest selection of new clubs to choose from?" or "Where can I rent a piano?" should be answered by your ad. Think to yourself, "What's my unique selling proposition and how can I out-sell the competition?" Then, put the answers to those questions in your copy.

Bigger means more space, and more space means more room for copy. Don't be afraid to put a lot of information in the ad. Fill it up with facts. Research shows that ads with lots of text draw a larger response by a ratio of more than two to one.

Of course you're going to include your company name, your product and services, and your hours. Here're a few more things that can convince a buyer to come to you:

- **Reliability**. Include years in business, experience, size (the Bay Area's Largest Carpet Salesroom!), licenses, certifications, degrees, awards, and so on. Mention insurance, bonding, and guarantees.

- **Authorized Sales and Service.** State the name brands, trademarks, manufacturers, and companies you deal with. When it's appropriate, make clear that your employees have had special training, for example, include "Adobe Authorized Trainer."

- **Financing**. Let the customer know if you accept checks and credit cards. Is other long-term financing available? Do you have a lay-away plan?

- **Completeness of Line and Service.** Tell the prospect that you have the

Big bold type, reversed out of a black bar, works well for this ad

Advertise close to home

One of the key factors in a customer's decision of where to buy is how far away your business is from their home or office. The Small Business Administration confirms the importance of distance with these findings:

- The average independent store draws the majority of its customers from less than a quarter of a mile away

- The average chain store draws most of its customers from not more than three-quarters of a mile away

- The average shopping mall draws its customers from as far as four miles away

Your location is all-important. Don't just list your street address. Help your customers by referencing cross streets or landmarks. If people have commented that they've had trouble finding you, include a map in your ad.

Late-breaking developments

In their search to keep up with other advertising mediums, the Yellow Pages have been introducing new services. One service that every guerrilla should investigate is the electronic Yellow Pages. This feature puts a toll-free number in each ad that prospects can call for more information. The recording at this phone number can be updated monthly to reflect any changes to your location, hours, inventory, and so on. An ad that's not current is going to irritate your customers and cost you sales.

Simple line art can dress up any ad

largest selection. Inundate them with facts on types, scope, variety, inventory, capacity, and cost. Emphasize the quality and availability of service.

If you have two strong selling points, consider placing two ads. For example, one ad might proclaim "Open 7 Days a Week" while the other announces "Free Pickup and Delivery." Whatever you decide to include, make your ad look classy. This is not the place for dumb cartoons or pictures of your pets. Keep the tone warm but professional. Remember, the readers are ready to buy, right now! Convince them to buy from you.

Working within the guidelines

The Yellow Pages have some stringent ad guidelines. The guidelines are there to create a consistent look through the book. This can make it harder for your ad to make a lasting impression.

When you call about placing an ad, you'll talk to a sales rep. Use this rep as a resource, but don't be intimated by the guidelines. Ask for advice on designing an ad that grabs attention while staying within the specs. Don't ignore the simple distinctiveness of an interesting border. Inquire about the use of colored inks, usually red, green, and blue. Check on the requirements for illustrations. PhotoDeluxe Business

Edition is great for trying out various type, illustrations, and colors against the soft yellow background typical of most Yellow Pages.

Plan ahead. Unlike other types of print advertising, Yellow Pages ads have a definite and early deadline, and it's usually a few months before publication. If you miss the deadline, you miss your opportunity for an entire year. Don't let ineffectual ads continue to run because you forgot or didn't have the time to place a new one.

From one into many

In the olden days, there was just one Yellow Pages. In most communities to-

Although this ad is smaller than the full dimensions available, the line art jutting out of the box makes it appear larger than the surrounding ads

Metered ads

One effective way to test Yellow Pages ads is to participate in metered ads. Metered ads involve placing an ad that contains a unique telephone number that is remote call forwarded (RCF) to your office or store. The RCF number isn't given out by directory assistance or included in other print advertising. You can be sure that any call received at this number is a direct result of the Yellow Pages ad. Each month the telephone company provides a summary of the calls made to that number.

Yellow Pages terminology

Although some of these terms seem self-explanatory, you want to be ready to "talk the talk" when you deal with your local sales rep. Here's a cheat sheet for Yellow Pages lingo.

- **anchor listing**—The tag line at the end of your Yellow Pages entry that references your display ad. For example, "See our ad on page 79."

- **bold listing**—An alphabetical listing printed in bold lettering.

- **Certified Marketing Representative (CRM)**—An advertising representative certified by the Yellow Pages Publishers Association to place, design, and implement ads for local and national advertisers.

- **heading**—A classification (category, section) in the Yellow Pages that groups different types of businesses.

- **in-column ad**—An ad that appears alphabetically within the columns, under the appropriate business classification (instead of elsewhere on the page or on another page).

- **utility publisher**—A company that publishes the Yellow Pages for a telephone company. There are also independent publishers that are not related to any particular phone company.

The thick, bright-red border on this ad captures the reader's attention

MARKETING TIPS

◆ Bigger is better

◆ Fill the copy with facts, not adjectives

◆ Get a toll-free number or invite collect calls

◆ Keep track of entry deadlines

◆ Unless your ad dominates the heading, don't refer customers to the Yellow Pages

day, this is no longer the case. Like other businesses, the Yellow Pages has learned to target specific markets and demographics. In addition to the standard consumer Yellow Pages, there are now Business-to-Business Guides, Industrial Purchasing Guides, the Asian Yellow Pages, Community Directories—the list grows every day. If you're trying to choose one over the other, check for your competitors. When the same directory goes to both consumers and businesses, you're probably better off in the consumer Yellow Pages. It's of-

ten more effective to recruit business customers through direct mail.

Testing the ad

Unlike newspaper, magazine, and classified ads, Yellow Pages ads don't lend themselves very well to testing. The ad only runs once a year and there are lots of rules to follow. You can conduct an informal poll by asking customers if they saw you in the Yellow Pages. What did they like or dislike about the ad? What could you do to make the ad more effective? Was key information missing? When the next year's ad rolls around,

Pick the right colors for your ad

If you have the option to use color in your Yellow Pages ad, use PhotoDeluxe Business Edition to try out different effects. Even if you can't use colored text, you can preview what the ad will look like on the soft yellow paper used in most Yellow Pages directories.

To change each text object's color, double-click on the text and select a new color from the Text Tool dialog box

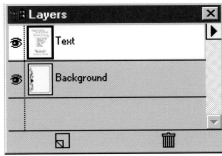

incorporate their suggestions (if there's been very little response, it's probably time to drop the ad).

Another new feature in some Yellow Pages is the pages of coupon promotions found in the middle or back of the directory. Since this has not been around very long, there's not yet much feedback on coupon profitability. If your company regularly offers coupons, try calling a few of the coupon pioneers already in the directory, and ask about their results. A good guerrilla always learns from those who have gone before. ■

These two variations try out different colors for the phone numbers

Direct Mail *105*

Direct mail

Taking it to the streets

D irect mail is the perfect guerrilla marketing tool. It's cheap, it's targeted, and it's easy to test. Everyone uses direct mail, from the lowly hobbyist working out of her garage to giants like Proctor and Gamble. In direct mail, you can compete with the big guys. Inside the mailbox, all envelopes are equal.

Use direct mail postcards to keep your customers informed of changes

WE ARE MOVING!

Monday, February 8, 1999

Leonardo's Art Supply

987 Artist Place
Easel, LA 12345

800-555-ARTS

Direct marketing consists of three simple steps: contacting targeted prospects, making an offer, and inviting prospects to become customers.

This topic discusses general information about direct mail marketing. The remaining topics in this section provide examples of how you can use PhotoDeluxe Business Edition to create several types of direct mailings.

What is direct mail?

The term "direct mail" refers to everything from an insert inside a credit card bill to a full-color, 60-page catalog from Pottery Barn. As the name implies, it's any offer received in the mail that requests a response. This response can vary from a call for more information to an immediate order. Many direct mailings offer special discounts or include discount coupons. Their anticipated response is to draw the recipient into the company's place of business or make a direct sale. Direct mailings don't have to contain a solicitation. Sometimes they're an invitation to a special event, a listing of upcoming classes, or a thank you for a referral. Often the

What should you test?

Here're a few things to test in your direct mailings:

- motivators
- prices
- letter lengths
- first class versus third class
- different lists
- method of delivery
- method of ordering
- number of enclosures
- postage paid versus required postage
- envelope color and treatment

Direct mail reminders provide a service for your customers

It's time for your pet, Lionel, to have his yearly check-up and rabies vaccination.
Please call 555-7342 at your earliest convenience to make an appointment.
Thanks,
Dr. Garnder, DMV

Valley Vets
means healthy pets

direct mail piece serves to simply remind people that you exist and want to do business (or more business) with them.

Selecting the right list

Unlike direct mail giants, your direct mail marketing goal is not to reach everyone. In fact, guerrilla law suggests that you do exactly the opposite, that is, go for the individual. To do this you have to focus your energy and dollars on a very small, very precise, target audience. You don't have to find this audience yourself. There are people out there who do this for a living.

Renting lists is a major source of income

The keys to successful direct mailings are picking the right list, presenting a great offer, and constant testing.

Thank you notes, such as this one created from template thanks01, are the most appreciated direct mailings

for many publications and direct mailers. These businesses generate substantial income by offering their lists to other marketers at a cost ranging from $50 to $1000 per thousand names. Managers are constantly updating the lists to create more and more specialized groups. Since you're not preoccupied with volume, these specialized lists are like manna from heaven to smart guerrillas.

The list business is a scientific attempt to divide the population into ever more meticulously defined segments. Today, it's possible to get a list for an unbelievable number of groups. Here're a few of the possibilities:

- Women in Kansas that own pickup trucks and drive them more than 250 miles a week

- Subscribers to *Sports Illustrated* that live in Manhattan and don't belong to health clubs

- Doctors who have purchased medical software programs using the Web

- Alternative families living in Idaho with more than six children

- Teachers who can't afford to use anything but recycled materials

MARKETING TIPS

◆ Don't forget your own customer database when drawing up a list

◆ Get fresh lists—at least 20% of the people on a list move every year

◆ Make the offer irresistible and easy to respond to

◆ Test everything, but only one thing at a time

Finding your list

To locate a list that meets your needs, start by looking through the SRDS (Standard Rate and Data Service) direct mail catalog. With more than 10,000 mailing lists, this volume has a list for almost everyone. Simply weed through the categories until you find the list that covers the people you're selling to. (If you don't know who this group is, stop now and go back to your marketing plan. You must have a carefully defined audience to make direct mail work.)

The Keepers of the Lists

While you can locate the list in SRDS, you need to rent the list from a broker. List brokers are paid by list managers and they don't cost you anything. Good list brokers are an invaluable source of information and should never be overlooked as a source for advice and investment experience. The following are just a few of the list brokers resources available to you:

American Business Lists
5711 South 86th Circle
Omaha, NE 68127
(402) 331-7169

Direct Media
200 Pemberwick Rd.
Greenwich, CT 06830
(203) 532-1000

Names and Addresses
4096 Commercial Ave.
Northbrook, IL 60062
(708) 272-7933

Directory of Mailing Lists Companies
Published by Todd Publications
18 N. Greenbush Rd
West Nyack, NY 10994

Finding quality and affordable day care is rare enough. Finding it right in your neighborhood is AMAZING!

- Entering Our 12th Year of Service
- Based on the Proven Summerhill Model
- Certified Early Childhood Instructors
- Serving Children from 3 months to 12 years
- Highest Rating from the American Association of Day Care Providers
- Sunflower limits its enrollment so that all children get individual, personalized attention
- Structured, yet exciting, projects help children acquire important social and learning skills
- At Sunflower, there is no distinction between play and learning!

Now Available!
Limited part-time and
full-time openings!

Self-seal mailers allow for photo-filled direct mailings as in this mailer using template nserv 08

You usually rent a list for one-time use. Once you get a response from a person on the list, that name belongs to you. Keep in mind that lists get stale and old very quickly. Keep careful records of which lists work for you, then periodically contact the list manager for updates. It's just smart economics to keep your lists current.

Creating an effective offer

No matter what type of package your direct mailing comes in, it always contains an offer. The goal is to make the offer so irresistible that the recipient has to respond, and the sooner

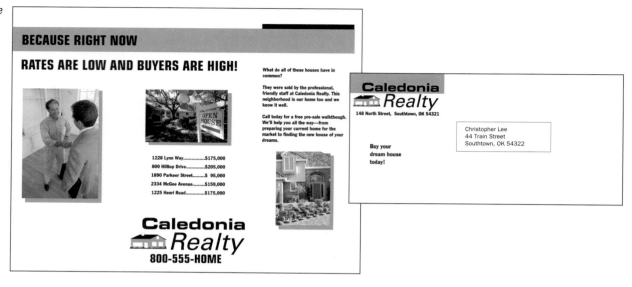

Self-seal mailers provide lots of information for little cost

BECAUSE RIGHT NOW

RATES ARE LOW AND BUYERS ARE HIGH!

What do all of these houses have in common?

They were sold by the professional, friendly staff at Caledonia Realty. This neighborhood is our home too and we know it well.

Call today for a free pre-sale walkthrough. We'll help you all the way—from preparing your current home for the market to finding the new house of your dreams.

1228 Lynn Way..............$175,000
800 Hilltop Drive.............$205,000
1890 Parkeer Street........$ 95,000
2334 McGee Avenue..........$159,000
1225 Henri Road.............$175,000

Caledonia *Realty*
800-555-HOME

Caledonia *Realty*
148 North Street, Southtown, OK 54321

Buy your
dream house
today!

Christopher Lee
44 Train Street
Southtown, OK 54322

Advantages of direct mail

Direct mail has several advantages over other types of advertising media. Using direct mail you can do all of the following:

- measure results accurately

- make the piece as terse or extensive as you want

- fine-tune your target audience

- create personalized marketing

- have unlimited testing opportunities

- develop repeat sales

- compete with the giants

the better. If you offer an expensive product or service, you might want to include a free estimate or sample in your mailing. Or the offer may require that the person come in for an appointment so you can make the sale face to face. Determining the offer may seem like the easiest part of creating a direct mailing. But, if the offer isn't effective, it doesn't matter how pretty the package is.

Testing equals success

Direct mail is such an open field that no one knows exactly why one mailing works and another doesn't. Research has shown that long letters do better than short ones, mailings received on

Direct response is different from direct mail

Direct response is a form of advertising that lets anyone respond to your ad. You pick the medium—newspaper, magazine, radio, or TV—and then take your chances. The majority of the people reached by the ad will not be interested in your product or service (this is where the big guys have the real advantage). Smart mail order guerrillas, however, have had success by turning this usually impersonal form of sales into a more intimate experience. Many have been able to attract and keep loyal customers who continue to purchase specialized items over a long period of time. If you have **a product that works well with mail order** (the critical component for success), and you're willing to put in the effort to develop a strong market base, you can translate direct response into a highly profitable business.

Tuesdays do better than those delivered on Thursdays, and adding a PS to a letter always increases the response. There is no rhyme or reason for these statistics, they just are. And all of them are backed by extensive testing.

Make sure that every piece you send out has at least one test on it. It might be color versus black and white, or one price versus another, or even different letter lengths. As long as you have about 250 people in both your control and test groups, you can run a test. It's probably overkill to test on more than 400 people.

Don't make the mistake of testing different audiences. For example, if you test the same piece using an urban zip code and a rural zip code, your results can be skewed by the differing lifestyles of the two groups.

To track your testing, put a 3-digit code somewhere on each piece. You can then tally results when you receive the card, order, or coupon. If the response is a telephone call, use two different 800 phone numbers or instruct the operator to ask for the code when taking the order. You must constantly test both the successes and the failures until you've found exactly the best direct mail strategy. ■

THE 60-30-10 RULE

◆ 60% of your direct mail marketing success depends on using the right list

◆ 30% depends on making the right offer

◆ 10% depends on a creative package

Postcards

Minimizing mailing costs

Postcards, of course, are not a guerrilla invention. (They're most likely a travel industry invention.) In the context of direct mailing, postcards are a guerrilla marketer's dream come true: an economical and powerful marketing tool that packs a full punch and costs only pennies. What more could you ask for?

This card uses a large postcard template. The original artwork was deleted and a patterned border was added to the back and front of the card.

Why and when postcards work

One of the best things about postcards is that they're cheap. You save on printing and postage costs. Best of all, you don't have to spend your Sundays folding letters and stuffing envelopes. You can probably do a postcard direct mailing for less than 40 cents a piece and that's a great deal! Stick to the basics of a focused list, an irresistible offer, and lots of testing, and you can conduct an extremely effective direct mail campaign using just postcards.

Postcards tend to be read or at least glanced at. People don't need to open an envelope or spend much time getting the gist of your message. Everything is right there with a simple flick of the wrist.

Use postcards to make announcements or get attention, but don't count on them to close a sale. Postcards are a good way to prompt prospects to make a call for more information, send in for a free sample, or come into your store or office.

Designing the postcard

To create a postcard, choose Projects > Promote > Direct Mail Cards and then choose the Postcard layout.

Postcards, like advertisements, only have a second to get the recipient's attention. They need to be flashy, entic-

One of the best things about postcards is that they're cheap.

KERRY FAMILY CHIROPRACTIC
456 Yucca Road, Spring City
NM, 12345

FIRST-CLASS MAIL
U.S. POSTAGE PAID
Permit No. 000
Spring City, NM

Carol Simmons
235 Summer Street
Portland, OR 12345

Free Back Care !

KERRY FAMILY CHIROPRACTIC

free!

*Back care
for
one month!*

Bring this card to our office
and enter our contest for
one month of free back care classes.

555-BACK

*Use a bright colored
paper stock and one ink
color to cut down on
printing costs yet still
produce an attention-
grabbing postcard*

ing, inviting, informative, and succinct. Don't waste any space on either side of the card, but don't stuff it so full of text and graphics that the message gets lost.

Attract attention with a dynamic headline that emphasizes the benefit to the recipient. Since you're sending to a focused target group, you can even personalize the appeal with such statements as Save Money on Your Next Toyota, Ideal for New Parents, or You're Already Approved for a Home Equity Loan.

Even within the size limits of postcards, you can make the message convey a specific tone. For a weekend sale, create a sense of urgency. For a grand opening, use expansive language. For a private sale, adopt a more intimate tone. You don't need to go far to research the variety and diversity of direct mail postcards; the postal service probably delivers several to your doorstep each week.

Make it easy for the prospect to take action. Emphasize your phone number or address and include hours and directions

Tempting customers with a Secret Sale

Many guerrillas have found the Secret Sale to be a powerful tool for bringing current customers into their store. A Secret Sale postcard offers existing customers a discount of 10% to 60% on everything they purchase in one trip to the store. The trick is that the amount of the discount is unknown. You can include the discount on the postcard under a rub-off seal that must be removed at the cash register. If that's too expensive, have the customer draw a discount coupon from a large bowl as they check out. Most people cannot resist the suspense or the promise of a 60% discount on their next purchase. (As a smart guerrilla you know, of course, that you better offer a lot more 10% than 60% discounts!)

when they would be useful. Use visuals to spur action and make it clear what you want the customer to do. For example, you could add clip art of a phone to emphasize a phone number or include a map with well-known landmarks.

Printing the postcards

You can add impact to any postcard by printing on colored stock or using two colors of ink. You might even test a card with a full-color picture of your product (color increases readership by 41% and raises the inclination to buy by

Postcards are versatile

Postcards are a good way to introduce your product or your service. They're also helpful in reminding current customers of your existence. Here's some effective use for postcards:

- familiarizing a new target audience with your company
- announcing sales
- introducing new products
- offering discounts to special customers
- inviting entries into a drawing or contest
- notifying customers of a change of address
- drawing customers to a grand opening
- sharing a good review
- publicizing an award or other recognition
- sharing recent successes

26%). To keep the costs down, modify photos from your other advertising pieces by adding a new border or applying a special effect to the text.

When you're ready to print, the templates are automatically set to print on Avery postcard stock. For more information, see "Using Avery paper stock" in the Labels topic.

Increasing response with testing

Because postcards are inexpensive, you don't need much of a response to make the mailing worthwhile. Still, you want to maximize the impact of each mailing. Test the card in both black and white and color and combinations of ink and stock. Modify the offer in two different mailings. Use two different headlines. Vary the motivators such as a discount, a free prize, or a contest. Experiment with different sizes. Try out several

Edit the artwork layers on a template

When you want to use a template for the layout or size but create an original design, you can delete some or all of the template artwork. You must exit a guided activity and merge the layers before changing any artwork.

This example used the news01 template from the Projects > Promote > Direct Mail Cards guided activity as the basis of this postcard. The template was opened and then exited by clicking the Done tab.

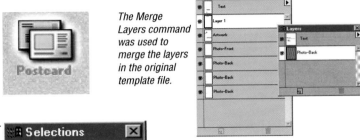

The Merge Layers command was used to merge the layers in the original template file.

The selection tools (the Color Wand for areas of solid color and the Object Selection tool for text areas) were used to select the artwork that was then deleted using the Advanced > Tools > Delete tool.

lists and alternate the days when you mail the cards. Remember, however, only test one thing at a time. A rather modest increase in response rate will more than pay for all your testing.

To track the postcard's effectiveness, make sure it contains a code that can be easily found by the recipient. Ask for the code when they call. If the desired action is to come to your place of business, request that they bring the card when they come in. You can even reward them by promising, "Bring this card with you to get an additional 10% off!" ■

The logo was dragged into the postcard from the Hold Photo folder (alternatively, you can use the File > Open command) and the new text was added using the Text tool.

The postcard was then printed using the Send & Save > Multiple on a Page guided activity. The Avery postcard template was automatically chosen as the paper type. For more information, see "Using Avery stock" in Labels.

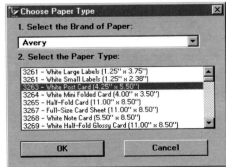

Self-seal mailers

Offering more in a small package

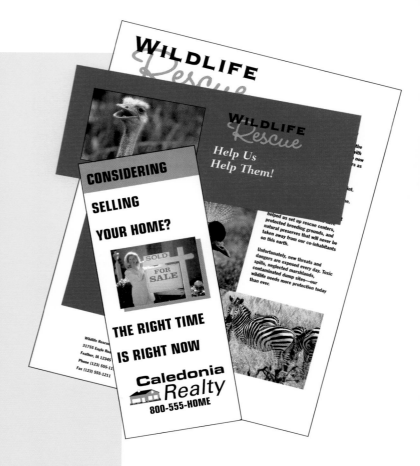

Suppose you want to use direct mail but have more to say than will fit on a postcard. Well, one easy solution is to use a self-seal mailer. These threefold, single sheets are useful for a myriad of purposes—introducing a company, announcing expanded services, small catalogs, nonprofit solicitations—just about anything that gets mailed to targeted audiences.

What's a self-seal mailer?

Self-seal mailers have four areas: top, center, bottom, and inside. The outside top is for your irresistible teaser. The outside center is for the address. The outside bottom contains some incentive to open the mailer. Your message fills all three inside sections of the mailer.

To use a self-seal mailer template, choose Projects > Promote > Direct Mail Cards and then choose the Self-seal Mailer layout. When you're ready to print, the templates are automatically set to print on Avery Self-Seal Mailer stock. For more information, see "Using Avery paper stock" in the Labels topic.

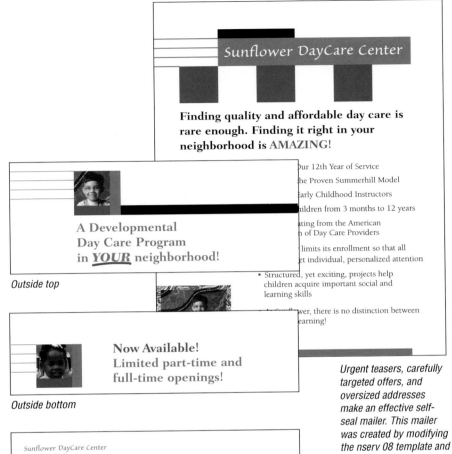

Outside top

Outside bottom

Outside center

Urgent teasers, carefully targeted offers, and oversized addresses make an effective self-seal mailer. This mailer was created by modifying the nserv 08 template and adding art from the Sample Photos gallery.

The most
important
part of a
self seal
mailer is
the teaser
on the top
panel.

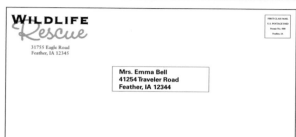

A beautiful photo and white type on a solid color make this teaser jump off the page

The crucial come-on

The most important part of the self-seal mailer is the top. This is where you get your critical three seconds to draw in the prospect. Make sure this teaser states the benefit to the reader in no uncertain terms: How to Triple Your Profits in One Month, Need $50,000 Right Now?, Get the Medical Care You Deserve, I've Never Been So Happy in My Life, Critics Call it the "Show of the Century," or something equally intriguing. Keep the message short and to the point. Don't underestimate the power of testimonials in your teaser, they can lend a personal and inclusive tone.

One effective technique is to use a bright, inviting, solid color for the top of the mailer. Then, reverse the type in white or black to make the message jump out. If you're going for a refined look, you can use a more subtle combination. A photo or drawing can also be compelling. The important thing is to get the recipient's attention and get them to unfold and read the rest of the mailer.

Don't waste the address space

The center section of the mailer is for the address. That doesn't mean that you can't add some interesting touches in this space. Your logo and return address will take up the upper left corner, but

WILDLIFE
Rescue

The heart-gripping beauty of an eagle in flight...the extravagant display of a strutting peacock...the tenderness of a mother osprey with its offspring. We need your help now to preserve these natural w... more than a memory.

Naturalists and historians a... agree that we are at a turni... We must act now to preserv... wildlife for the generations...

Through your generous gifts... have made great strides in t... decade. Your contributions... helped us set up rescue cen... protected breeding grounds... natural preserves that will never be taken away from our co-inhabitants on this earth.

Unfortunately, new threats and dangers are exposed every day. Toxic spills, neglected marshlands, contaminated dump sites—our wildlife needs more protection today than ever.

Everyday,
more and more come
closer to extinction...

Wildlife Rescue
31755 Eagle Road
Feather, IA 12345
Phone (123) 555-1111
Fax (123) 555-1211

Carry through your teaser on the outside bottom panel

What's the normal percentage of return?

One well-kept guerrilla secret is that there is no "normal" rate of return. Your product, audience, location, and marketing determine what is normal for you. Once you've determined your own norm, set about improving it.

Most households receive about 104 pieces of direct mail each week. About 40% of it is from national advertisers, 25% is from local advertisers, and 20% is from mail-order firms. You can see that you need to be very creative and aggressive to make your mark in direct mail. On the other hand, some non-profits report that they raise 90% of their funds through direct mail.

MARKETING TIPS

◆ Grab attention with a teaser

◆ Use oversize addressing

◆ Include the offer in the headline

◆ Repeat the basic mailing (with slight variations) several times

◆ Urge immediate action

Help with headlines

The headline makes or breaks your direct mail campaign. If you're stuck for a headline, think of them as falling into several categories. Which tone are you going for? Here're some possible headlines for a child photography studio.

- **News**. "Now There Are Two Convenient Jan Jordan Child Photography Studios."
- **Featured Benefit**. "Save up to 25% on Our Most Popular Photography Packages."
- **Boastful**. "Voted Best Child Photographer in the Bay Area!"
- **Command**. "Get Your Holiday Photos Taken Now."
- **Emotional**. "Don't Let the Memories Slip Away."
- **Curiosity**. "Have You Looked at Your Child Today?"
- **Testimonial**. "Everyone asks, "Who did that wonderful portrait?""
- **Prediction**. "Five Years From Now, You'll Be Happy You Took the Time."

that still leaves a lot of room. Experiment with additional photos, another teaser, or swatches of color.

Here's a Top-Secret Guerrilla Tip: One of the easiest ways to gain the goodwill of the receiver is to use oversize addressing. Yep, just increasing the size of the address type can improve response rates. Everyone likes to see their name in print, and the bigger the better. Don't be above appealing to the vanity of your potential buyers.

Repetition is the key

Because of the way it's folded, the bottom of the self-sealer is seen before the

The inside of self-seal mailers can present text horizontally or in three vertical columns

inside. This space provides another opportunity to urge the reader on. You can give a hint of what's inside with a teaser such as "Free Ticket Enclosed" or "Special Sale for our Premier Customers." You can also use this area to recap the essentials of the offer or announcement, "Sale Hours 9 am to 5 pm, July 21 and 22 ONLY!" or "Transitions: An Exhibit of Italian Folk Art, now on display at the Galleria Sophia."

An offer they can't refuse

Once it's opened, the first place the recipient's eyes should go is to the headline. In fact, the best headline is one that makes the offer. For example, "Watch the Playoffs On Your Own New Big-Screen Television," or "Order Today and Receive a Second Book for Half Price." Sometimes it's better to ease the customer in. If you're using a gentler approach, be sure and begin the offer by acknowledging the needs of the customer. Don't try to persuade them as to why they

DESIGN TIPS

◆ Use bright, vivid colors for the top panel

◆ Add photos or color to the address section

◆ Isolate the headline with size or font differences

◆ Group important information with bullets

Always end your offer with a request for a specific action.

need your product or service, instead demonstrate how it meets their needs. Make sure you introduce the product in the first few lines of the offer. If a prospect has to read too long without grasping what's being offered, you've probably lost them. Always end your offer with a request for a specific action. Don't imply what you want the buyer to do—make it crystal clear. Include an order form, a telephone num-

ber, or an invitation. Give exact instructions on how to proceed, for example, "Call Now!", "Come In Today!", or "Use this Handy Response Card to Receive More Information."

Tracking responses

A direct mail campaign is not made up of one mailing. The most successful campaigns go on for years. They are honed to precision by tracking the results of previous mailings. Which headlines are

working? Which mailing lists produce the best returns? When is the best time to mail? Is it more effective to include an order form or a telephone number? Does a lower price bring more response? These are the kinds of questions that you need to test, over and over again. On a per-sale basis, direct mail is the least expensive method of marketing. While the overall costs can be high, if it works for you, it's inexpensive. ■

Create interesting edges for your photos

Open the photo you want to use. When you're adding an edge effect, it's best if the photo has a little extra space around the main focus

Use the Rectangle tool in the Selections palette to select the photo area you want to keep unchanged

Click the Invert button on the Selections palette so that the area around the edges of the photo is selected

Click the effect you want to use. This example uses the Advanced > Effects > Special Effects> Elegant > Colored Pencil tool

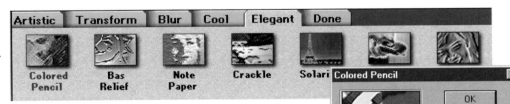

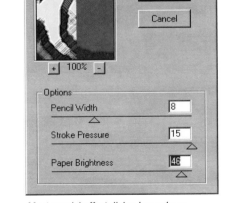

The Colored Pencil effect works best in areas with dense colors

Most special-effect dialog boxes have preview windows where you can see how the effect will look before you apply it to the entire photo

Classic package

Keeping tradition alive

Traditionally, direct mail meant using the postal service to solicit orders from a targeted audience. The "classic direct mail package" consisted of a letter, envelope, brochure, order form, return envelope, and other inserts. Today, direct mail encompasses almost anything you send to a targeted audience, whether by regular mail, email, fax, or the Web.

Getting the envelope opened

Because of the volume of direct mail that goes into every home each day, you have about three seconds to get the recipient to open your envelope. If the envelope doesn't demand to be opened, the rest of your package is not important since at worst it will end up in the trash or at best in the recycling bin.

There're lots of different ways to get the envelope noticed. If you're mailing to executives, keep it formal. Use white or buff envelopes and pay to have them hand-addressed or typed. (Labels don't go over well with executives.) Use first class stamps and don't include a return address. The mystery of the sender tends to get a very high response rate. If your mailing is small and you really want to impress, have the piece delivered by Federal Express. Make sure the return on the offer is worth the cost before you become this extravagant.

If it's a more general or informal mailing, use bright color envelopes and oversized addressing. But the key to envelope-opening is an irresistible and compelling teaser. Don't be shy about putting your benefit out there for everyone to see. "Free gift enclosed" is sometimes enough, but "Incredible money-

FINANCIAL CARE, INC.
DOWNTOWN

Investment for Individuals

VOLUME 25, NUMBER 6   JUNE 15, 1999

The Year 1999:
How it will effect you?

Back in the 1940's, when they were working on the first vacuum-tube computer, the pioneering engineers at IBM didn't think about the year 1999. Who knew, during that war-filled time, if humans, let alone the machine they were designing, would still be around 60 years later. Yet, here we are, with less than 18 months to go before the familiar prefix, 19 disappears forever.

In the

FINANCIAL CARE, INC.

DOWNTOWN

66 West Seventeenth Street, Goldbar, MN 12345
(voice) 123-555-1267 (fax) 123-555-1266

May 30, 1999

Mr. Glenn R. Stanek
Deni Construction Company
1344 Orland Drive
Nashville, Tennessee 000898

Dear Mr. Stanek,

WE CAN SAVE YOU TIME AND MONEY!

In today's bustling world, no doubt the Deni Construction Company keeps you very busy. We also realize part of assuring security for your here to provide you the personal ultants, is a specialist in the needs of e options, and then sit down with estment and financial plan.

s, mutual funds, or other investment

FINANCIAL CARE, INC.

DOWNTOWN
66 West Seventeenth Street
Goldbar, MN 12345

Mr. Glenn R. Stanek
Deni Construction Company
1344 Orland Drive
Nashville, Tennesee 000898

Richard Thompson, President

P.S. Glenn, we are sending this letter on the recommenda of service to you. Mr. Hursh is a satisfied customer of Fin take a moment now to call Ms. Ryan at 1-123-555-1267 s offering you financial security today! Thanks again.

Investment for Ind

A variation on the classic package: newsletter, personal letter, hand-addressed envelope, and brochure

FINANCIAL CARE, INC.
DOWNTOWN

Investment Brokers
Investment for Individuals

ONE (123) 555-1267

WWW.FINCARE.COM

Developing your own mailing list

While you may find it useful to buy specific mailing lists, perhaps the most important list is the one you generate yourself. If you have the soul of a guerrilla, you've been saving the names of prospects and customers since day one. Keeping a customer is much easier than finding a new one. Make repeat sales to existing customers as important a part of your marketing strategy as getting orders from hot prospects. Follow these tips for building a mailing list:

- Every time someone calls about your business, get their name. Offer to send a brochure or other information and you've got their address as well.

- Whenever a customer leaves something with you, for example, an item to be repaired, be sure you get their name and address.

- Keep all contents and sweepstakes entries so that you have the name and address of everyone who entered.

- Install a suggestion box. Not only will this help you find out what your customers think, but it's also another source for names and addresses.

- Give a free newsletter or catalog to anyone who gives you their name and address.

- Design an insert so that customers need to fill it out and return it to take advantage of your offer.

- Include a warranty card in your product. A warranty card collects not only names and addresses but other valuable marketing information as well.

- Create a new customer kit that contains coupons, a catalog, and a questionnaire.

- Place a large container, such as a fishbowl, on your counter and invite customers to drop in their business cards for a free drawing or a future discount.

Use this mailing list as the jumping-off point for your mailings. It's also handy for sending sale notices, holiday cards, thank you cards, and reminders.

saving offer inside" is better. A personal message such as, "Learn How You Can Double Your Profits" often does the trick. But best of all is a photo of the offer right on the envelope. And don't forget the back of the envelope; 75% of recipients read it first.

Composing the letter

Create a letter that's as personal as possible. Be sure you use a mail-merge program to address the recipient by name and include their company or business name in the body of the letter. As usual, you need a catchy headline to get and keep the prospect's attention. One sure-fire technique is to open by describing

the customer's problem. Remind them of how the problem won't go away and may be getting worse (Tune Up Your Fireplace Now—Before the Winter Nights Arrive!).

Go on to explain how your company can solve the problem. Get the benefit into the first few lines of the letter even if a detailed explanation comes later. Mention how easy and affordable your solution is. It's always a good idea to include some testimonials to back up your claims. Then start pushing the offer. Refer to rising prices and busy schedules. Reiterate what a great deal it is. Guarantee your work. Provide a

Marketing Tips

◆ Make the letter as personal as possible

◆ Don't underestimate the power of the PS

◆ Do anything to get the envelope opened

◆ Choose the right list

◆ Follow up every mailing

Direct mailer's checklist

- Does the outside of the envelope demand that it be opened—immediately?
- Is the letter the first thing you see when you open the envelope?
- Does the number one benefit hit you between the eyes?
- Does the number two benefit follow closely behind?
- Does the letter discuss the reader's needs, product benefits, features, endorsements, and ways to respond?
- Do the graphics support the copy?
- Does the package flow?
- Is there a reason to act now?
- Is it easy to respond?
- Would you respond?

personal guarantee of satisfaction to re-assure the customer that you stand by your company and are not a fly-by-night organization.

End your letter with the importance of immediate action. You might put a time limit on the offer or give a discount or bonus for immediate orders. If your let-ter is longer than one page, use two separate sheets, not two sides of one page. Two individual pages have a proven higher response rate.

Making the most of the PS

Surprisingly, postscripts are the most often read part of direct mail letters. Use an energetic tone as you repeat the benefit and urge a response. Give pre-cise instructions as to what the pros-pect should do: peel off a label, fill out a form, or return the postage-paid card. Use boldface type or a second color to emphasize your most impor-tant points. If the mailing is small enough, a personally written postscript or an individualized Post-it note can be very effective.

What else goes in the package?

Depending on the nature of your business or service, you may or may not include additional pieces in your package. Some direct mail entrepreneurs live and die from a business reply card (BRC). Others use coupons, tickets, complimentary slips, or invitations to solicit action. Whatever you include, make sure your package flows and all the components repeat the essentials—the problem, the solution, the benefit, and the required action.

Following up on mailings

No matter what the contents of your package, following up with repeat mailings is an essential component of direct mail success. In earlier times, direct mail meant a letter. Now it means an introductory package, anywhere from two to five follow-up letters, a phone call or two, and a final direct mail letter. Some guerrillas send out direct mail packages weekly or monthly. It's important to make each offer slightly different, yet keep the same familiar message. ■

Fade back a photo

One way to personalize stationery is to add something interesting to the letter area. In this case, the logo photo was repeated. The photo needed to be faded back so that the typed text would be legible.

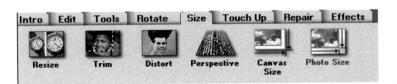

Open the photo. If you need to change the photo size, choose Advanced > Size and select the Resize, Trim, or Photo Size tools.

To fade back the photo, click Special Effects > Transform > Make Transparent.

Type a lower number into the Opacity box in the dialog box. Check the photo to see the effect. If it's not what you want, enter a new value. Click OK when you're satisfied with the amount of fade.

Opacity 20%

Opacity 30%

Opacity 50%

Reminders

Providing a gentle nudge

One form of direct mailing that's a cornerstone of service industries is the reminder card. Usually printed as postcards, reminders serve as an impetus for your regular customers to make their checkup appointments, review their insurance policies, or sign up for an event before the deadline slips by unnoticed. Reminders are the grease that keeps long-established relationships running well.

Send reminders well ahead of critical deadlines. This reminder was created using the remind01 template from the postcard layouts in the Projects > Promote > Direct Mail Cards guided activity.

Who should send reminders

If you're a doctor, dentist, veterinarian, haircutter, bodyworker, or mechanic, reminders are probably already a part of your periodic mailings. You've worked out a schedule of visits with your clients and they have come to expect a timely reminder from you.

But there are many other businesses that can use reminders to put their names in front of their customers. Retailers can send reminders of the number of days left in a sale or the number of shopping days until Christmas. Florists can send reminders of birthdays or anniversaries for which the customer has sent a gift of flowers in previous years. Photographers can send reminders of the time that's elapsed since the last family portrait. Investment companies can send reminders for annual portfolio reviews. Suppliers can send reminders that special orders have arrived. And anyone who teaches can send reminders to former students of new classes and enrollment deadlines.

Clip art can reinforce a friendly message

Designing a reminder

The only point of a reminder is to get the customer to call and make an appointment or come into your place of business. You don't need to spend much time composing the message, a catchy headline and the word Reminder just about says it all. To use PhotoDeluxe Business Edition reminder templates, choose Projects > Promote > Direct Mail Cards, then choose the Postcard layout and choose a reminder template. When you print using the Multiple Print guided activity, the correctly sized Avery post-

card will be preselected. For more information, see "Using Avery paper stock" in Labels.

You will want to personalize the card with the patient's or customer's name and a description of the type of visit that's needed. For example, "Jim, it's time for your annual physical," "Your pet, Brigid, needs her rabies vaccine," "Your Nissan is due for its 25,000-mile service," or "Your custom-designed oak headboard has arrived." The most important thing about a reminder is to enter the phone number in big type

Using databases effectively

Gone are the days when you could keep track of your loyal customers and hot prospects by jotting them in a Rolodex. Although you can build a database on 3 x 5 index cards, the age of relational database marketing is upon us. As a forward-looking guerrilla, you need to develop and maintain a database as one of the linchpins of your marketing strategy.

Databases start with a simple customer list, but using the power of the computer you can recombine and extrapolate amazing information about your customers. Think of every entry as an individual, not a statistic. Make an effort to get beyond name and address and take that extra step of learning about interests, needs, and desires. Build a relationship with each client. For example, if you have a customer who bought printer paper last month, you could contact them this month for a refill order. If you know certain patrons are crazy about garlic, you can make sure you notify them about the annual garlic week at your restaurant. Anticipating your customers' needs makes for a lasting and satisfying seller-customer relationship.

Computers today are so inexpensive that most small businesses use them to keep their databases. Programs such as FileMaker Pro are popular and powerful database applications. If you're a retailer, you probably have a POS (point-of-sale) system that supports computerized information capture.

The goal of any database system is to find out what your customers want and need and then make it easy for them to let you fulfill those desires. A guerrilla, understanding the power of a database, keeps records of every purchase, why and when it was sold, and when a repeat sale or related purchase may be necessary. When a special shipment comes in or a new product is introduced, it's a cinch to create just the right mailing list for a promo or reminder. Here's some powerful information you can get from your database:

- **Refine the demographics of your audience.** Where do they live and what do they have in common? What cars do they drive? What hobbies do they have? What do they read or do for leisure?

- **Categorize their habits.** By studying the data you'll see patterns that you can use. If parents always buy a certain kind of diaper, notify them when a related product comes in. Find out what kinds of movies your customers prefer and why most people rent on Friday evenings.

- **Figure out what they want.** Are customers buying a lot or a little of certain products? Are there specific hours that your store should be open? Do you repeatedly run out of items at a regular time of the week?

Use humor and fun art to get the message across

Valley Vets

4134 First Street

Milltown, PA 07243

Susan Swan
123 Turtle Creek Court
Milltown, PA 07244

Time for me to visit Valley Vets!

It's time for your pet, Lionel, to have his yearly check-up and rabies vaccination.
Please call 555-7342 at your earliest convenience to make an appointment.
Thanks,
Dr. Garnder, DMV

Valley Vets
means healthy pets

MARKETING TIPS

◆ Use humor or a personal tone in reminders

◆ Keep a detailed database of all customers, purchases, and individual needs

◆ Tell the client why they need to act now

◆ Track students to remind them of new or related classes

(large enough to be read by someone calling from their cell phone while they're on their way to somewhere else).

Graphics on the front of the card are one way to get the postcard noticed. Since these cards can often be overlooked, use brightly colored stock. Colorful clip art can also help get the recipient's attention.

A good place for humor

Reminders are one place where you don't have to worry about first impressions. Since you're sending them to people who are already customers, you can afford to be a bit more casual. Many reminder cards use cute teasers on the address side, such as "If You Can't Read This, It's Time for Your Eye Exam!" or "Post This Notice Where Your Owner Will See It." Here's one place where you can let your imagination run wild. ■

Change text into a graphic

By default, the text in a PhotoDeluxe Business Edition file is always in the Text layer. It's easy to edit this text using the Text Tool dialog box and move or resize the text using the Object Selection tool. But there are times when you may want to do more with text. For example, you might want to apply a special effect or edit individual words or letters. To do this, you must put the text on an ordinary layer. The easiest way to do this is to save the file in a different format from the PhotoDeluxe format (.pdd), such as the JPEG or TIFF formats. Once your file is saved in the new format, the text is treated as any other graphic and you can manipulate it using most of the PhotoDeluxe Business Edition tools.

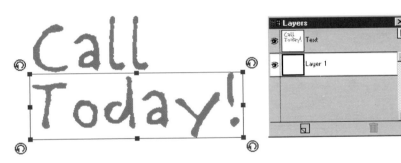

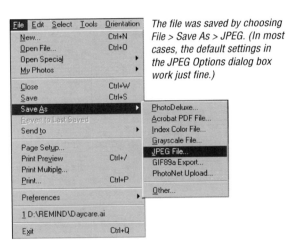

The file was saved by choosing File > Save As > JPEG. (In most cases, the default settings in the JPEG Options dialog box work just fine.)

In this example, a new file was created and the text was added using the Text tool. The text appears in the Text layer. To select this text, you use the Object Selection tool.

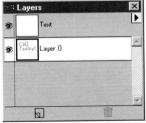

When the JPEG file is opened, the text appears on Layer 0. The text is now ready to be manipulated as a graphic.

For this reminder, the color of several of the letters was changed using the Advanced > Tools > Color Change tool. No selection is necessary because the Color Change tool selects and changes the color in one step.

Invitations and thank-yous

Treating customers right

Wise guerrillas know the importance of keeping in touch with their customers. In addition to solicitations, direct mailings are an effective way to build and maintain loyalty with your customer base. Two of the most welcome uses of direct mail are for invitations and thank you notes.

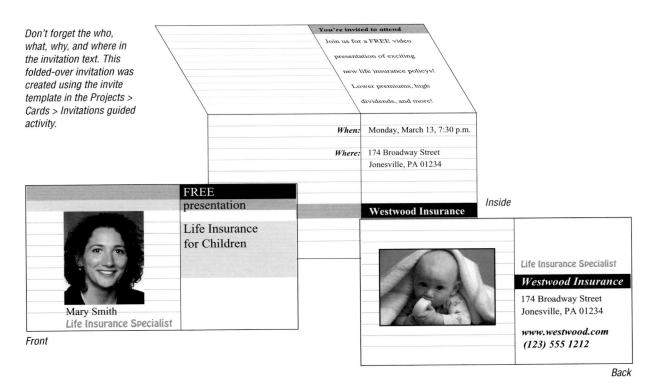

Don't forget the who, what, why, and where in the invitation text. This folded-over invitation was created using the invite template in the Projects > Cards > Invitations guided activity.

You're invited to attend

Join us for a FREE video

presentation of exciting

new life insurance policys!

Lower premiums, high

dividends, and more!

When: Monday, March 13, 7:30 p.m.

Where: 174 Broadway Street
Jonesville, PA 01234

Inside

Westwood Insurance

FREE
presentation

Life Insurance
for Children

Mary Smith
Life Insurance Specialist

Front

Life Insurance Specialist

Westwood Insurance

174 Broadway Street
Jonesville, PA 01234

www.westwood.com
(123) 555 1212

Back

Let the customer know how attending the event will benfit them.

Invitations and thank-yous

141

Selecting templates

Invitations can come in many shapes and sizes, and PhotoDeluxe Business Edition has a variety of templates to meet almost any need. For simple events (and to save money), you can send postcard or self-seal mailer invitations. To select a postcard or self-seal mailer invitation template, choose Projects > Promote > Direct Mail Cards and then select the Postcard or Self Seal Mailer layouts. You'll find two postcard invitation templates and one self-seal mailer invitation.

For more elaborate events, you can customize side-fold and top-fold cards. To create cards, choose Projects > Cards > Invitations. You can choose from top fold and side fold templates. All of these templates can easily be turned into thank you notes as well.

Postcards, self-seal mailers, and invitations are all preset to print to specific Avery papers. For more information, see "Using Avery paper stock" in the Labels topic.

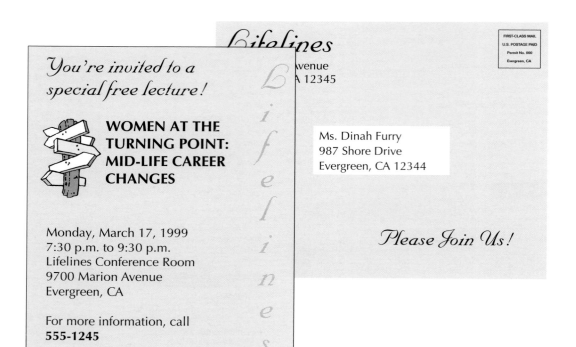

You're invited to a
special free lecture!

**WOMEN AT THE
TURNING POINT:
MID-LIFE CAREER
CHANGES**

Monday, March 17, 1999
7:30 p.m. to 9:30 p.m.
Lifelines Conference Room
9700 Marion Avenue
Evergreen, CA

For more information, call
555-1245

Lifelines

...Avenue
...A 12345

FIRST-CLASS MAIL
U.S. POSTAGE PAID
Permit No. 000
Evergreen, CA

Ms. Dinah Furry
987 Shore Drive
Evergreen, CA 12344

Please Join Us!

*Using clip art on a
colored paper
stock is a good
way to cut costs*

Making customers feel special

Anytime you can draw a prospect into your office or place of business, you've got a potential sale. Providing interesting, necessary, or entertaining information at the same time is an added bonus. Use invitations to invite customers to events such as lectures, presentations, classes, demonstrations, parties, or special-interest groups. Unlike sales and promo pieces, the invitation doesn't need to dazzle your audience with a grabber headline. Most of the recipients are probably existing customers, so you can expect that they're already interested in your company, service, or product. You can still use an attention-getting vocabulary, such as Free, Fun, and Fascinating, but let recipients know up front that this is an "invitation" (in other words, a no-pressure, enjoyable event). Use phrases like "You're Invited," "Come Join Us," or "Learn Everything You Ever Wanted to Know about Life Insurance" on the front side of the card or envelope.

Invitations don't need to be folded cards with matching envelopes. For larger, less formal mailings, use the postcard layout in Projects > Promote > Direct Mail Cards. This card uses the thanks01 template.

Thank you
Danke
Gracias
Merci beaucoup
TAKK

Way Out Travel
136 Summer Street
Riverview, KS 01234

Way Out Travel
We appreciate your business.
800-555-UFLY

143

Your message can be brief, but don't neglect to include the all important five: Who, What, Where, When, and Why. Let the customers know how attending this event will benefit them. Promise that they'll go away with something useful, for example, "Packing for a Trip," "How to Choose a Decorator," or "Making Your Exotic Plants Thrive." Let customers know if there will be any cost or if they need to make reservations or send an RSVP. You should always include complete instruc-

tions on the invitation. Don't make it necessary for your customers to call to get essential information or directions. Do include a phone number, however, for those who will get lost on the way.

Don't forget to say thank you

Thank you mailings are appropriate whenever you have a pleasant or suc-

Creating a compliment slip

PhotoDeluxe Business Edition includes templates for a special kind of invitation/thank-you. These coupon-sized cards are called compliment slips (or comps). To use these templates, choose Projects > Forms > Compliment Slips.

Comps have a wide variety of uses in guerrilla marketing. You can include them in the mailing that accompanies a request for information, send them along with a free sample, or use them as thank you notes. Many businesses also keep on hand a supply of blank compliment slips printed with their logos. They use the slips to write a quick personal note to attach to interesting articles or information they know their customers would appreciate.

144

If your business is one that provides premiums at the conclusion of a successful sale or negotiation, comp slips can be attached as gift tags to the premium. For example, a travel agency might give customers a bon voyage bottle of wine with a personalized comp slip tied to its neck. Or a lumber company might give free screwdrivers with large purchases and attach a personalized thank you comp slip to the handle.

This compliment slip uses the compsl05 template from Projects > Forms > Compliment Slips

cessful interaction with a prospect or client. You may want to thank someone for responding to an advertisement, visiting your company or store, or attending a class or demonstration. And, of course, you want to thank clients and customers when they have made a purchase or referred someone to you. Thank you cards are an integral part of any business and are never overlooked by vigilant guerrillas.

Thank you cards are the nicest way to remind customers of your existence. Be creative and you can send cards quite frequently. For example, one enterprising guerrilla got the name and address of every person who came in to look for a new car. The very next day he sent them a thank you card. This was a personal

How to...

Use preprinted papers

Many copy centers, stationery stores, and mail order companies sell paper with preprinted borders. You can use these papers with PhotoDeluxe Businss Editon.

Choose File > New to create a new document that's the size you want for your final document. These papers are appropriate for single-sided stationery, flyers, and newsletters.

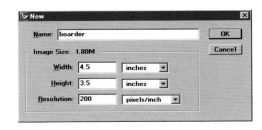

message, describing the exact car, with the specific features that they'd been interested in. If you bought a car from this salesman, you were on his permanent mailing list and received a card from him every month. These mailings were not strong-armed sale incentives; instead, they reminded clients that they were important to the salesman. A more subtle message suggested that they might want to refer friends to him. This may sound excessive, but this salesman sold more cars in one day than others did in two weeks! Most sales were to repeat and referral customers. Remember, the reward for a good direct mailing campaign is long-term, loyal customers. Invitations and thank you cards are a good way to cultivate this loyalty. ■

Measure the width of the preprinted border and subtract that value from all four sides of the document. For example, if the border is 1/4 inch, allow that much extra space all the way around the card when you enter text.

Add the type using the Text tool

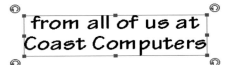

Print the card using the Send & Save > To Printer > Multiple on a Page guided activity, then cut the cards to separate them

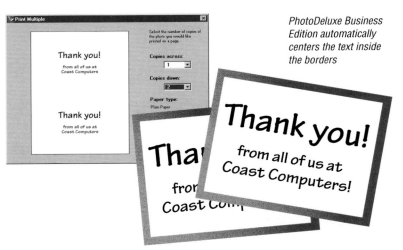

PhotoDeluxe Business Edition automatically centers the text inside the borders

Inserts

Leveling the playing field

I nserts are one arena in which David can truly compete with Goliath. To the recipient, all inserts are the same whether they come from Chevron or from your guerrilla enterprise. People tend to be very democratic with inserts. All of them are treated equally—if they don't leap out and engage the prospect immediately—they're history.

BRCs offer something in return for the customer's willingness to send in their name and address

Never mail out anything without including an advertising insert for one of your products.

Inserts

147

Doing your research

Although inserts are relatively low cost to produce, you still don't want to waste your hard-earned guerrilla dollars. As with any form of direct mail, the quality of the mailing list is more important than the quantity. If 20,000 people get your insert, but none of them are interested, it won't turn out to be an economical campaign after all. So, be sure you choose the right distribution program, geared to the demographic group most likely to want your product.

Inserts are very effective when they are sent as part of a package. Search for a marketer who's reaching the people you're interested in and then insert your message along with theirs. Everybody wins. If your insert accompanies a package that contains merchandise, check that the merchandise is something that will increase the response to your offer.

All kinds of inserts

There are several different types of advertising that are referred to as inserts. Their names reflect how they're delivered to the prospects.

Ride-alongs. Ride-alongs are pieces included in packages that are already being mailed to customers. They can be included in your own mailings, or you

Solicit specific customer information on a subscription BRC

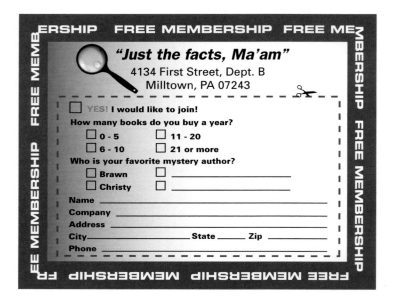

can contact a company that has a related product and arrange a deal with them. For example, if you run a gardening service, ask a local gardening supply store to include your insert in their statements. Your company wins with new clients, and their company wins when your clients order supplies.

Free-standing inserts (FSIs). Free-standing inserts are ride-alongs that come in your daily or weekly newspaper. In major markets, these inserts are produced by huge companies that want to blanket a large area. This nontargeted approach is not useful to most guerrillas.

You can, however, use FSIs on a smaller scale. Approach your local newspaper and offer to print a high-quality, color insert that they can stuff in the paper (they may not have thought of inserts as a source of revenue yet). You can limit the distribution by putting the FSI only in papers delivered to selected zip codes. To spread the cost around, try forming a group of neighborhood companies and go in together on an FSI. This is a great marketing tool for local retail stores, contractors, optometrists, restaurants, or anyone else who wants to get known in a specific neighborhood.

Direct mail terminology

"Direct mailese" is a little-known language spoken among a very small tribe in several major financial centers throughout the world. Here's your handy, pocket-sized translation guide.

- **alternative delivery**—any delivery system that is not the postal system. Alternative delivery companies usually deliver directly to the prospect in a polybag. Great for free samples:

- **bounce back coupon**—a coupon in a direct mail piece that's redeemed by mailing it back to you.

- **business reply card**—a direct mail response card that's enclosed in a direct mail package (letter, card deck, catalog, etc.). The BRC is used to respond in some way to the offer. In most cases, a BRC has a postage-paid address so it's easy for the prospect to drop it in a mailbox.

- **co-op mailing**—A set of direct mail inserts from several advertisers mailed in a single package, for example, Val-Pak and Carol Wright mailings.

- **one-step**—a mailing that asks for an immediate order. The anticipated response is that the customer buys the product. A two-step offer generates leads and the expected response is a request for more information.

- **ride-along**—a direct mail piece that's inserted into a package someone else is mailing out.

- **self-mailer**—a direct mailing that is folded to create its own envelope. Self-mailers are usually stapled closed or sealed with a tab. They are less expensive to produce than a full-scale direct mail piece and require less postage.

- **statement stuffer**—the advertisements or direct mail offers included with bills and statements sent out to existing customers or to another company's customers.

Mailbox inserts. No matter where you live, your part of the country has a company that brokers direct mail inserts. These brokers collect a number of local advertisers that want to share in the cost of sending an envelope full of offers and coupons to everyone in a neighborhood. You may recognize these packages by the names "Val-Pak" or "Mailbox Values." Contact a broker listed in the Yellow Pages to take part in such a distribution or get together your own assortment of local merchants.

Card decks. Card decks are a collection of postcards mailed as a set and usually targeted to small businesses. Each deck

10 rules for an effective BRC

Depending on your product, including a business reply card (BRC) in your mailing or in a card deck may be just the thing you need to encourage customers to respond. For some people, having to make a call or stuff something in an envelope is just too much work, but they can take the time to check off a box and drop a postcard in the mail. Don't make it too easy, however, or you'll get responses from people who aren't really that interested. Here're some hints on creating BRCs:

1. Make sure the offer is incredibly clear.

2. Avoid stilted and legalistic language. Write with energy and personality as one human being to another.

3. Keep the benefits up front.

4. Emphasize that there are no risks and restate your guarantee.

5. Include checkboxes for ordering options. When there aren't any options, put a pre-checked box in front of the word "YES."

6. Encourage readers to call by highlighting the 800 number.

7. Put all important information on the front of the card.

8. Use graphics to guide the reader and lure them into action (a big red arrow or clip art of a phone helps focus attention).

9. Attach a stub. A receipt of mailing is a useful reminder if they've ordered something.

10. Name the card appropriately. Instead of an "order form," try "response card," "action card," or "upgrade card."

Inserts are used to promote almost everything. You need to make a strong impression amidst the clutter.

contains from 50 to 200 cards. The front of the card is the advertisement while the back contains the business reply card. It doesn't cost much to be included in a deck, and it's possible to reach as many as 100,000 businesses for less than three cents a card. Card decks are very tightly targeted. For example, there are The Business and Management Books card deck, the Biochemistry and Molecular Biology card decks, the Teacher's card deck, and so on.

Creating inserts

PhotoDeluxe Business Edition has several templates that you can use for creating everything from coupons to business reply cards. You can also combine templates to get just the insert you need. For example, you can use a flyer tem-

Checking for multiple responses

There are some dishonest folks out there who increase their flea market and used bookstore inventories by responding to card decks for free samples. When you first start using card decks, be sure and check for multiple responses from the same name or address. Eliminate these names immediately and you'll save yourself a lot of trouble later on.

plate and turn it into a full-page FSI, or you can use a direct mail card and turn it into a business reply card.

The guidelines for creating inserts are the same as for other direct mail pieces:

- grab them with a headline that shouts benefits

- keep the copy simple and friendly

- show a picture of your product

- emphasize words like FREE, GUARANTEE, NO RISK TO YOU

- ask for an action

- provide an 800 number

- supply a postage-free mail back card

- offer a free sample of your product or at least a free gift for responding

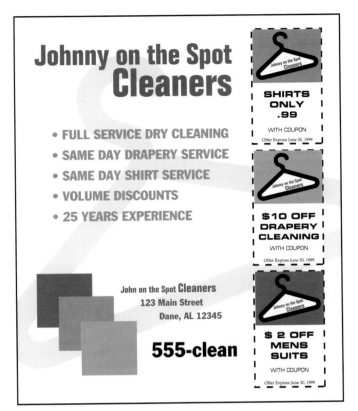

Increase the value of your insert by including coupons. In this example, the coupons were added by modifying the TravPromo 2 template from the Travel gallery in the Projects > Promote > Flyers guided activity.

HILL
for Mayor

Come to the town meeting
and hear the candidates debate.
10/17 at 7 p.m. at the Priest Valley Grange

Inserts intended to be slipped under windshield wipers (such as this one created from the coupon16 template in Projects > Promote > Coupons) should be simple and focused

MARKETING TIPS

◆ Choose the right broker or distribution program

◆ Allow inserts inserted with products six months for full distribution

◆ Test 10,000 inserts in each program

◆ Break up large insert groups into several keys for testing

◆ Test at least ten programs at a time

Check with the distributor or broker you're going to work with and then create an insert that's the maximum size. Test copy that you know already works from your own mailings and advertising. Include a five- or six-digit code on the insert so you can track the responses. This is especially useful if you'll be including the same insert in more than one insert package. You need to know which distributions are working for you.

Taking the mail out of direct mail

Not all direct mail pieces go through the post office. Many cost-conscious guerrillas hire friends or kids to distribute inserts to neighborhood mailboxes, slip them under windshields on parked cars, or leave them under doormats. One step up from the personal delivery method is to use an alternative delivery company. These businesses deliver products in polybags that are hung from doorknobs. Alternative delivery is being used by catalog makers, magazines,

Convert a color photo to one color

Often it's too expensive to produce a full-color insert. Converting a photo from color to black and white, however, may result in a loss of impact. To save money on printing costs and still get the best effect, consider printing a photo using a single color.

Visualize what you want the finished piece to look like. This insert depended on a simple, clean design. To keep the focus on the face, the background was eliminated from the photo.

First, the background was selected using the Color Wand selection tool. Pressing the Delete key eliminated the selected area. The image was then converted to various shades of gray using the Advanced > Effects > Color to Black & White tool.

Next, the photo was reduced to two colors (black and white) using the Advanced > Artistic > Posterize tool. (Since the photo contains only shades of gray, selecting 2 levels in the Posterize dialog box made all the pixels in the photo either black or white.)

This insert was designed to be duplicated using color Xerox. Blue reproduces well in color Xerox and also added to the patriotic appeal. The Advanced > Tools > Color Change tool was used to turn the black areas into bright blue.

and newspapers. These vendors can offer virtually unlimited ride-along opportunities for their advertisers while reducing their own mailing costs. Rates for alternative delivery are calculated on the size of the insert or product sample and the number of households reached. Unlike second and third class postal mail, alternative delivery can guarantee delivery dates and cuts down on undelivered mail. It's a great way to put your direct mail insert or sample into the hands of potential customers. ∎

Inserts

153

Everyday Advertising *155*

Online marketing

Taking advantage of the Web

As we approach the millennium, our concepts of marketing, advertising, selling, service, and customer relationships are undergoing a profound change. Many of the old models of marketing are being updated to take advantage of the age of online access. Forward-looking guerrillas are going online because that's where the customers are.

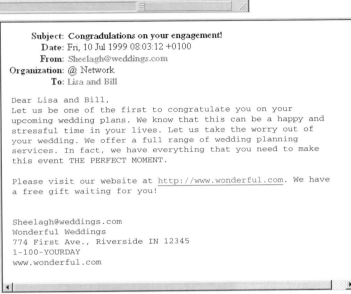

Effective email advertising needs a snappy subject line and must be directed at a very focused audience. Use the body of the email to direct recipients to a Web site.

Providing a Web advantage

Two of the most common uses of the Web are advertising your company and selling products through an online storefront. Advertising on the Web lets you reach thousands of customers who would otherwise never be aware of your company's existence. Selling on the Web allows you to provide longer hours and faster delivery. This combination of increased exposure and improved customer service goes a long way toward increasing your bottom-line profitability while shrinking your marketing and overhead costs.

Before investing in online advertising or marketing, consider if it is an appropriate tool for your company. Will going online offer special advantages to your customers? Will 7-days-a-week, 24-hour access make a significant difference? Will people be able to get information more conveniently than from other sources? Will you be able to provide more up-to-date information or faster technical support? Can you provide related information that would otherwise not be available? You need to understand why it makes sense for people to do business with you online and provide incentives that will keep them coming back.

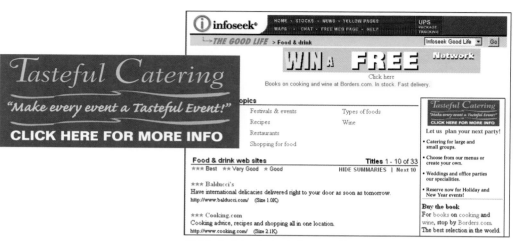

Invest wisely by placing buttons on sites that draw from your target audience

158

7 strategies for online advertising

1. Use a strong title.

2. Use people talk to help bridge the electronic gap.

3. Use power words that convey benefits.

4. Make it easy to respond by setting up an email reply or including 800 numbers.

5. Offer something free (this always works!).

6. Check your ad regularly and change it frequently.

7. Code responses to track effectiveness.

The most important aspect of online marketing is locating your audience. Luckily, online buyers have already sorted themselves into topic-specific groups. Begin your marketing research by getting demographic information from the online services and locating newsgroups and forums that focus on topics related to your business. The audience potential of the Web is enormous, but concentrating on a smaller, well-focused target group is always the best bet for guerrilla marketers.

Advertising on the Web

Placing a Web ad can be as simple as repurposing your printed classified ad or as complex as designing an animated

Understanding Internet services

Although Internet has become almost synonymous with World Wide Web, there are different Internet services. To help you keep them straight, here're a few of the most frequently used terms:

Internet (Net)—an international data communications network that links thousands of smaller computer networks.

World Wide Web (WWW or Web)—information stored on Internet servers (in the form of Web sites) that is accessed using a browser and navigated by using links.

online service—a commercial BBS offering a lot of information and services (including email and Internet access). Online services, such as AOL and CompuServe, can accommodate thousands of users at one time.

bulletin board service (BBS)—any computer system and software that accepts phone calls from another computer. A BBS is usually organized like a miniature online service and serves individual cities, particular subjects areas, or other specific communities.

discussion group—an electronic message center on an online service, BBS, or the Net that contains messages focusing on a specific topic.

forum—a discussion group located on a commercial online service (and some bulletin boards) that usually supports chat rooms, message centers, libraries, and conferencing.

newsgroup—the Internet (Usenet) version of a message board.

banner. Web advertising falls into five general categories.

Classified ads—Online services and Web directories offer both free and paid classified sections. In general, paid ads are more effective since free areas tend to be very crowded. Classified ads appear as a list of titles. Readers browse through the list, opening those titles that interest them. Responses can be by way of Reply email buttons or you can include your 800 number in the ad. To get the most out of your classified ad, give it a creative and benefit-filled title and keep the text short and to the point.

Storefronts should be designed for speed and the customer's convenience

Discussion group ads—Participating in discussion groups is a good way to generate leads. If the group is primarily a message center, be discrete in promoting your product or service. A simple referral in reply to a request for advice can be very useful. Some forums and newsgroups are more commercial in nature. For example, the AOL Business Strategies Forum has advertisements for accounting and other business-related services. Any newsgroups with "for_sale" in their name are devoted to advertising, but most are for individuals selling personal items. Check that commercial ads are allowed before submitting an ad to a newsgroup.

Graphical ads—The most visual form of Web advertising is the use of banners, buttons, and billboards. These graphical (and often animated) ads appear on most commercial Web sites. While they attract a lot of attention, banners and buttons can be expensive (for information on bartering for graphical ad space, visit the Internet Link Exchange at www.submit-it.com). Banners, buttons, and billboards have only one purpose—to get the reader to click it so that they move to your site. Bright colors, blinking text, and simple graphics do the best job of grabbing the reader's attention.

Banners should be bright, to the point, and compel the viewer to click

When paying for advertising space, aim for precision. Place your ads in discussion groups and on Web sites where the highest percentage of people seeing them will be likely prospects. Your money will be well invested if you spend less to reach a more focused audience.

Selling on the Web

Which method of online selling you choose depends on how much time, energy, and money you're willing to put into the effort. One of the first things you should consider is whether your product or service lends itself to online marketing. In most cases, retail products do better on the Web than services.

If you offer a service, create an informational Web site that prompts the prospect to call for a personal appointment. If you do decide to sell on the Web, you'll probably choose one of the following options:

Email marketing—You can choose to send individual emails or you can use bulk email to send promotional materials. Just as there are list brokers for direct mail, there are companies specializing in selling email lists. At its best, email advertising is fast, costs you nothing except your monthly Internet account fee, and can be aimed at specific individuals and groups. At its worst,

Shopping cart systems

If you plan to sell more than a handful of items from your storefront, you'll need to implement an automated ordering system. Shopping cart systems let customers choose items as they browse through the store. Each time they make a selection, the item is automatically added to an order form. Before completing the order, customers have the option of removing items, verifying quantity and cost, and choosing a shipping option. The order total is calculated automatically. Shopping cart systems cost from about $500 to $2500, but your ISP may have a licensed shopping cart system that's included in your monthly storefront rental fee. The cost of a shopping cart system is quickly absorbed by the increased sales generated by offering a convenient and fast ordering process.

DESIGN TIPS

◆ Add type effects to dramatize email subject lines and classified ad titles

◆ Animate banners and buttons

◆ Design the storefront for speed and convenience

◆ Use browser-safe colors

bulk email annoys recipients so much that they send you very nasty replies. It's especially important that you send to lists that you're sure will be interested in your product or service. The most important part of the email is the subject line, since this is where you get or lose the recipient's attention. Keep your messages short and use signature cards to make it easier to respond. Email can be an effective way to direct people to your online store or to offer customer support. Check with your ISP to find out more about programs that automatically check your mailbox periodically and then read and respond to incoming email (mailbots).

Online shopping malls—Many online services have directories devoted to retail marketing. These directories list your store along with up to 20,000 other companies. The advantages of shopping malls include high visibility and promotion, useful advice on designing the storefront, a large, captive sub-

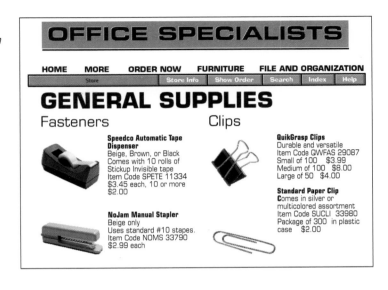

scriber base, and simplified online ordering. Disadvantages include the strong competition for attention, little control over the look and type of information you can include, and the cost (on CompuServe the least expensive mall option is $20,000 per year plus 2% of the sales). While general-interest malls, such as the Internet Mall, may not work for you because of their size and cost, you might try setting up your storefront on a regional mall geared toward a specific geographic area, or a mall devoted to a special topic such as real estate, financial planning, or food services.

Your own Web site—Setting up a storefront on your own Web site allows you the most control over design and presentation, but also involves the most work and money. In most cases, your ISP provides you with enough space to set up your storefront as part of your normal account fee, or you can rent extra space on a server if necessary. In addition to creating the pages, you need to be respon-

7 strategies for electronic storefronts

1. Choose the right location.
2. Make the store attractive, fun, and easy to navigate.
3. Make the store an information source.
4. Reassure customers about your permanence.
5. Pay attention to your store's activity.
6. Tell the world.
7. Follow up.

164

Make customer service a priority by including an easy-to-use, secure order form

sible for uploading and maintaining the site, creating an online ordering system, and promoting the store.

Planning and designing a storefront

An online storefront should be part of your integrated marketing strategy and reflect your business identity. Before you open your store, make sure you're ready to receive the expected amount of traffic and you've implemented an online ordering system. Establish your credit card accounts and shipping plans. And always include a way for customers to securely transmit sensitive financial information.

For a detailed discussion on organizing information, navigation devices, using text, including graphics, and creating links for Web pages, see the Web Sites topic. In addition to the usual Web site features, your storefront should include a registration page that allows you to collect data for your customer database. It's also a good idea to include a feedback area where customers can send comments, ask questions, or provide suggestions for improving the site.

Promoting the store

Just as you would with a physical store, plan a grand opening for your storefront. Give gifts to the first hundred visitors, send out press releases, place online classified ads, and post notices in forums and newsgroups. If your store is in a mall, try to get included in their What's New section or buy a banner or button on the mall's opening page. And don't forget offline promotion as well. Be sure to mention your store in replies to inquiries and include your store URL in all your printed materials.

Plan at least six weeks in advance to submit your store URL to the Web directories. Whenever you find a site that's likely to attract your target audience, ask if the site will put in a link to your store in return for the same favor from you. For more information on submitting your URL and gaining exposure, see "Register your site" in Web Sites. ■

Overlap text entries

When you want to rearrange the text or art on an image, you use the Object-order menu at the top of the file window.

This banner contains art and two different type text entries. The Text tool was used to enter the first line of text.

The Text tool was then used to enter the second line of text

The first line of text was then selected and moved by clicking the Bring to Front button from the Object-order menu.

The text was then dragged into position. The Object-order menu can also be used to move photos.

Flyers

Keeping it simple

Y ou may be wondering, exactly what constitutes a flyer? How is a flyer different from an insert or a brochure? Well, as in most industries, marketing terms vary from person to person and business to business. In this book, a flyer is arbitrarily defined as a one-sheet circular that contains a time-limited offer.

Labor Day Special

You save 50% on all software when you buy a new computer before September 6!

PCs and Macs—all the latest models Educational software—get a head start on the new school year.

The new iMac is now on sale at Office Specialists.

OFFICE SPECIALISTS

1-800-555-1334

123 Vista Lane, Storybrook, IL

Open 9 a.m. to 9 p.m. everyday!

Designing the flyer

As with all marketing pieces, even short ones like these, you need to first decide on the purpose and audience for the flyer (or flier—you'll see it spelled both ways). Most flyers have only one intention—to sell. Sell a specific product, service, or event. And sell it right now. Of course, buyers have another agenda. They want to know what's in it for them and they want to know it immediately. Keep the flyer headline focused on benefits and you'll have a good chance of getting the rest of the flyer read.

To get to the PhotoDeluxe Business Edition flyer templates, choose Projects > Promote > Flyers.

There isn't much room for copy on a flyer, so begin with one basic idea. Describe that idea in a single sentence. Then attempt to match the thought with a picture. This should get you well on your way to the headline and subhead. Keep the copy short and simple and use pho-

This flyer effectively illustrates the power of repetition in a design

tos as visual explanations of features or benefits. Always include captions under photos, and put your product or company name in the caption (these are called "selling captions" in the trade).

Make sure the flyer prompts for an instant action. Put a deadline on all offers and stress the urgency required to get in on this terrific deal. Make it easy for the prospect to respond by including all the essential information: the expiration

Flyers in the sky

A deli in Medford, Massachusetts prints up two-sided flyers. One side offers a discount on a sandwich. The other says, "Go Jumbos." They hand out the flyers before Tufts University football games. Guess which flyer gets held up every time the Tufts Jumbos score a touchdown?

Reinforce the flyer's message by using seasonally appropriate paper stock

date, your name, address, fax and phone numbers, store hours, and directions.

Dare to be different

Since the flyer will be handed out to lots of people or posted amidst a sea of other flyers, you'll want to do everything possible to make it stand out. You can print the flyer on brightly colored paper or use full-color photos on a subtle background. Or, experiment with borders or other graphic devices to attract attention to your message. As with inserts, the primary goal is to get the flyer to stand out from the crowd. So don't be shy; make your flyer as loud or dramatic as you dare.

While the major rush of sales will occur right after you've distributed a flyer, remember that you're also trying to develop a recognizable name brand. If

These days more and more flyers are being distributed using fax and email. Design electronic flyers in black and white with minimal graphics so that they transmit or download quickly.

you design a flyer than can be easily modified, creating future flyers that re-peat this theme will be a lot easier.

Distributing flyers

Flyers can be distributed almost every-where. They can be handed out on street corners or posted on bulletin boards (and telephone poles if your local legal regulations allow it). They can be slipped under windshield wipers or doormats. But even with such open dis-tribution, a little thought can help get your flyer into the right hands.

For example, if you do interior deco-rating, you might pass out flyers to

Features versus benefits

Throughout this book, it's suggested that you stress benefits. There is a distinction, however, between benefits and features. Features are the things that are inherent in your product or service. For example, steel-reinforced beams, vine-ripened tomatoes, or old-growth oak are features. Benefits are what the buyer gets from the product or service. The feature of steel-reinforced beams produces the benefit of "a tranquil sense of safety," vine-ripened tomatoes provide the benefit of "unbelievably fresh and juicy flavor," and old-growth oak assures that "your kitchen glows with the beauty of fine wood." It's relatively easy to define features, simply write down the important and unique aspects of your product or service. To discern benefits, have a virtual discussion with your customers. Look at each feature and then say, "You'll love this feature because...." The reasons you come up with are the benefits.

people as they enter a home or decorating show. If your specialty is repairing or renovating imported cars, put your flyers only on the windshields of foreign cars (there would probably be lots of them parked outside a car show).

You can even pick your street corners with an eye to a special event. If you own a pizzeria or a record store, for example, try handing out flyers to college students as they pour into a stadium for a game or concert. If you run a rafting company, position yourself near an outdoor gear store or show.

Barter with others for flyer space. This flyer, for example, could be given out at a local sporting goods store.

Introductory Offer

Get a Life!

Get a Life! Health Club is now offering an introductory 25% *off* the membership fee at our new facility in Greenfield.

We offer stationary machines, aerobic classes, and tennis courts.

555 A Street Greenville

Open 9 a.m. to 9 p.m.

Monday thru Saturday

Super Sale!
This Weekend
Only!
2/3 and 2/4

BF
Construction, Inc.
Your
key to
construction
success.

The unusual background and unique shape on this flyer attract attention and leave no doubt as to its message

How people read flyers

Would-be designers take heed. Someone has actually done research to define how people read flyers. It turns out that most people look at the headlines and subheads first, the special offer if it is emphasized next, the illustrations and captions, and lastly the copy.

Don't forget your own customers when you're distributing flyers. Put a flyer in every bag as you package customer purchases. A satisfied customer is one of your best advertisers. Hire a high-school kid to stand outside your store and pass out flyers during a sale. You'll get quite a few walk-ins if the flyer is effective. And don't forget to include a flyer in your own mailings.

To find out the best distribution locations, ask your customers if they came to the store in response to a flyer. If they say yes, ask where they saw or received it. Then concentrate on that location the next time you put out a flyer.

Adjust color using hue and saturation

Hue and saturation are two of the basic properties of color. Experimenting with these properties is an easy way to create color variations.

Open the photo and then choose
Advanced > Touch Up > Hue and
Saturation (alternatively, you can
use the Special Effects > Artistic >
Tint guided activity)

Bartering for space

Flyers work well as barter items too. Ask the owner of a related business if you can put your flyer on their counter in return for space in your store. Check out office or business locations near you that might use your service and ask if you can leave flyers.

If you run a deli, for example, ask the local office buildings if you can leave some flyers at the front desk, then offer businesses a discount on catered lunches. If you print your menu on one side and a special deal on the other, you might be amazed at the response you get. ■

*Lowering the hue and
increasing the saturation
and lightness tints the
photo brown while
keeping the original
highlights and shadows*

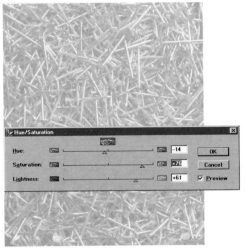

*Increasing the saturation
and lightness shifts the
color toward blue and
produces a slightly
transparent photo*

Product sheets

Getting specific

Within PhotoDeluxe Business Edition there are several specialized flyer templates. These templates are designed to offer information prior to making a sale. They appear under various names: product sheets, house sheets, and promo flyers. The only difference between these templates and other flyers is that they include more information and less hype.

Color and engaging photos add interest to this class description sheet

Using product sheet templates

In PhotoDeluxe Business Edition, you'll find templates for products sheets in several places. Some product sheets are included in the Projects > Promote > Flyers gallery, others can be found in the Projects > Cards > Album Pages gallery. Customized product sheet templates are also included in the Real Estate and Travel sections of the Projects > Business > Business Guides guided activities.

What's in a product sheet?

Product sheets contain descriptions, dimensions, performance results, exploded views, graphs, test results, comparison data, photos, statistics—all the information needed to help a prospect come to an informed decision. Think of them as a short form of a catalog. They provide a frame of reference that allows the purchaser to do comparison shopping.

All types of businesses use product sheets. Realtors use house sheets that are handed out to potential buyers or left in a display in front of the house. Consultants use product sheets to explain the purpose, features, and benefits

Provide a toll-free number

Ordering by telephone is perhaps the easiest way for customers to buy. Guerrillas know that supplying a toll-free number is a necessity for any business that attracts customers from outside their immediate area. According to AT&T, customers are seven times more likely to phone if a toll-free number is provided.

Acquiring a toll-free number is not an expensive proposition. Most of the major companies will set you up for a base charge of about twenty dollars a month, plus about twenty cents a minute. You don't need a special line for an 800 number and if your business moves, the number moves with you.

If you can get a number that is a word or phrase easily identifiable with your business, do it. Numbers such as1-800-FLOW-ERS have been very successful. But don't get too cute or complicated. And make sure it's a word that's easy to spell. Using a clever mnemonic can be a disaster if people can't associate the word with your business or tend to misspell it.

An 800 number often implies quick and convenient service and always means faster delivery. If you use an 800 number in TV or radio advertising, be sure you're ready to receive the volume of calls you hope it will generate. You might want to use a service bureau that specializes in direct response calls.

Your 800 number does not have to be limited to orders. You can set up an advice or information line and then take down the names of callers for your database. Or, use a special 800 number to introduce a new product. Promise a free sample to everyone who calls, and you'll be thinking like a real guerrilla.

Break up tables of information with photos and rules

An bfuil ólas agat ar vacation?

Now is the time and we have the fare!

Way Out Travel

136 Summer Street, Riverview, KS 01234

Call: 1-800-555-UFLY

IRELAND TRAVEL INFORMATION			
DESTINATION	CO. KERRY, IRELAND	CO. GALWAY, IRELAND	CO. DONEGAL, IRELAND
PER DIEM	FOOD/LODGING IR£ 50-80	FOOD/LODGING IR£ 40-60	FOOD/LODGING IR£ 30-50
WEATHER	WINTER 7C -9C SUMMER 14C-16C	WINTER 5C-9C SUMMER 12C-15C	WINTER 3C-6C SUMMER 10C-12C
MUST SEE	DINGLE PENINSULA RING OF KERRY	CONNEMARA ARAN ISLES	LOUGH DERG TORY ISLAND
ENTERTAINMENT	PUCK FAIR FESTIVAL FISHING	GALWAY ARTS FESTIVAL GOLFING	MARY OF DUNGLOE FESTIVAL
INSIDE INFO	DRIVE RING OF KERRY IN REVERSE ORDER	VISIT DUN AENGUS ON INISHMOR ISLAND	SLIEVE LEAGUE RIVALS THE CLIFFS OF MOHER
BEST BUY	QUILLS WOOLEN MARKET POTTERY	ARAN ISLES SWEATERS CELTIC JEWLERY	DONEGAL TWEEDS PARIAN CHINA

of their services. Travel agents use product sheets to describe the highlights of packaged tours. Computer manufacturers use product sheets to provide detailed specifications on their equipment. Tool distributors use product sheets to show performance benchmarks and compare test results. Food companies use product sheets to list ingredients and other nutritional information. Seed companies use product sheets to describe the environmental requirements for each fruit, vegetable, or flower.

Some businesses also put out another type of information flyer called a tech-spec (technical specifications) sheet. Product sheets and tech-spec sheets are often sent in response to direct mail inquiries. In business-to-business marketing, product sheets and tech-specs are directed toward the purchasing man-

ager. With this in mind, they are kept to a uniform size (usually 81/2 by 11) and three-hole punched so that they can be easily stored in a binder.

Organizing a product sheet

Often product sheets and tech-spec sheets are organized with a text section describing the product and its benefits and a separate section for technical

Customize your order form

Order forms are often a neglected piece of your marketing identity. It's relatively easy to design an order form that provides extra information for your customers. Often, an order form is the last hurdle between the customer and the order.

Make your order form as user-friendly as possible. You can include instructions or repeat your guarantee. Order forms are also a good place to highlight new products and current specials. If you're offering a free trial of a product, the order form is a great place to put this information.

Test out the ease of your order form by sitting down and ordering from yourself. Is it easy to find the identification code and price of your products? Does the form do the work of figuring tax and shipping charges? You may also want to offer different payment methods such as credit cards and direct deduction from bank accounts.

Consider allowing customers to fax in their order. If you do allow faxing, be sure to design a form that faxes clearly. The bottom line is to make ordering as simple and pleasurable as possible.

data. Rules are sometimes used to set off the data blocks. When writing the copy, it can be helpful to remember that the user as well as the buyer will be reading the product sheet. If appropriate, you can include suggestions for use and discuss the financial and environmental advantages of your product. Try to anticipate the questions of potential users and buyers and provide answers in the text and graphs.

When less is more

Nothing is more boring and more likely to turn off a buyer than a page of 8-point type, interrupted by a few headlines. Just because the product sheet contains a lot of information doesn't mean it has to be unimaginative. The

Photos and a tinted
background help to
lighten the look of text-
heavy product sheets

COAST COMPUTERS
PRICE LIST

Coast Computers offers the widest assortment of personal computers
in the West Bay Region. Individual systems are custom-designed to
fit your needs. All work is fully guaranteed. The Coast 3000, 2000,
1000, and 750E systems are available on a 36-month business lease
financed by North Financial Services.

COAST 3000
400 MHz
24X CD-ROM
56K Fax/Modem
8 GB Hard Drive
$2,959.00 or
$65.00/mo.

COAST 2000
300 MHz
24X CD-ROM
56K Fax/Modem
4 GB Hard Drive
$2,259.00 or
$50.00/mo.

COAST COMPUTERS

800-555-COMP

4422 Software Drive, Tampa
Fax: 800-555-7894
www.coastcomputers.com

old adage, "one picture is worth a thousand words," is good advice when it
comes to product sheets. Let photos do
much of the work. Use close-ups if necessary and show the product in use. Include a photo of your manufacturing
facilities, especially if this is one of your
major selling points. If you are selling
custom work, try to show the product
installed in a store or home. Creative
placement of photos can go a long way
toward breaking up streams of data.

Keep your name up front

Because a product sheet is presenting a
lot of information about the product,
it's smart to remember that after they
have the facts, prospects will want to
get in touch with you or your sales rep-

Make sure
your
identity
stands out
from the
data.

This template, prodsh1, found in Projects > Card > Album Page provides a good format for product sheets

Golf Bag
12345
Handcrafted vinyl bag with 3 outside pockets for easy storage of gloves, balls, and scorecard. Comes in black and brown. $199.95

Pierce Pro Golf Balls
12346
A core made of a responsive formulation of polybutadiene and a high performance cover makes this the ideal ball for all golfers. Set of 12..............................$35.00

Biodegradable Golf Tees
12347
Eliminate tee litter and protect our woodlands with these no petro-chemical or dyes tees.
1000..................................$13.00 per M
20,000..............................$11.00 per M

page 1

MARKETING TIPS

- Make sure the information is useful

- Use technical language and abbreviations sparingly

- Isolate contact information from other data

- Include photos to create a more user-friendly product sheet

resentative. Make sure your identity stands out from the data. Arrange the contact information in a convenient location. Your name, address, email address, phone number, fax number, toll-free ordering number, and Web site should be clearly set apart from the other copy. It's not a bad idea to repeat this information on both sides of a double-sided product sheet or on each individual page of a multiple-page product sheet.

Where have all the product sheets gone?

Because you often distribute product sheets freely, it's often hard to track where they go. Sometimes it's impossible. For example, house sheets may be picked up by anyone from a display in front of a property that's for sale. But if you come in contact with the person receiving the sheet, ask for their card, or keep a mailing list handy. This is especially important if you're giving away sheets at an open house, conference, or trade show. A highly trained guerrilla, such as yourself, never misses the opportunity to follow up with those interested enough in your product to request this kind of detailed information. ■

Create an order form

One way to create an order form is to start with a scan of a generic order form from your local stationery store. Open the scan in PhotoDeluxe Business Edition and modify it, adding your logo and business information. Order forms can be a good place to advertise overstocked items or those that sell only during certain seasons.

First, create the graphics you want to add to your order form and save the files in the Hold Photo folder

Next, scan in the generic order form and save that file in the Hold Photo folder

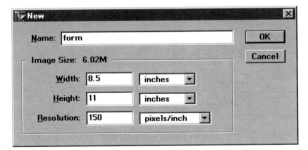

Choose File > New and enter the dimensions of your order form, usually 8.5 inches by 11 inches

Drag the order form and graphics out of the Hold Photo gallery and place them in the new file. You can also add additional text. If you want to keep the forms in a binder, leave room on the left side for the binder ring holes.

Signs
Attracting attention

Signs covers a wide range of marketing materials. They can include everything from 3 x 5 cards posted on bulletin boards to 44-foot banners plastered to the outside of your building. (In fact, they can even be your building if you go for outdoor paint jobs.) Whatever their size, the main purpose of all signs is to identify and position your business and generate walk-in traffic.

The Perfect Moment...

Wonderful Weddings
1•100•YOURDAY

Make the type on banners as large as possible

Positioning signs

If you have a store or office, you're already familiar with the way signs can influence would-be or repeat customers. First, there is your outside sign, which hopefully becomes a familiar landmark to passersby. This sign can be anything from a simple announcement of your name to a huge whale painted on the outside of your aquarium. The faster your sign communicates your positioning, the better. If you're located on a main freeway, as many as 50,000 people may see your sign every day. No true-blood guerrilla could ignore an opportunity like that!

On a busy street, you might consider erecting a sign that you change daily. If you're clever enough in your choice of witty or sage pronouncements, this sign will become a regular part of commuters' lives. Many will even look forward to seeing what you're up to for today.

◆ Keep the sign copy to three words if possible

◆ Stick with clear, easy-to-ready type

◆ Limit punctuation and don't use question marks

◆ Try black and white for a distinctive sign

◆ Use graphics instead of words

Rules for signs

All signs, whether inside or outside, have the same rules. Use this checklist before you hang any sign.

- Proofread exhaustively. You should check spelling and then have someone else check it. Mistakes do happen and are embarrassing and a turnoff to customers.

- For positioning signs, make a sign you can commit to. Spend enough money to make a great sign, then leave it alone.

- For window signs, posters, and bulletin board postings, change the sign frequently. Keep the message the same but rekindle interest by adding a new twist.

- Keep the message short. Drivers or passersby have only a few seconds to glance at the sign. Ten words is the maximum, six is even better, and three is the best.

- Check the zoning regulations for signs and banners. Then make the biggest, most obvious sign you can.

- Don't trick your customers by putting up a Going Out of Business Sale (if that is not the case). It's not a very encouraging message and people don't appreciate being duped.

Galleria Sophia
Contemporary Italian Art

The clean, classy look of this side reflects the modern art gallery inside

Window signs are appropriate for information that changes frequently

This is a great way to establish a relationship and hopefully convert some of those commuters into customers.

In a mall, office complex, or shopping center, the power of your sign is intensified by its location. But the plethora of signs can also have a distracting effect on customers' eyes. You need to be sure that your sign stands out from the clutter and quickly and accurately reflects who you are and what you do.

Window signs

Then there are the signs you put in windows or on stands outside your location. In addition to identifying and positioning your business, these signs also work to encourage people to stop and look (and hopefully come in and buy). Window signs don't necessarily need to be advertisements, although a blown-up ad does make a good window sign. They should, however, reflect your other advertising. Your ads make an un-

Words that persuade

The following list contains some of the most persuasive words in the English language. Put three of these together and you've got a great sign.

you	money	save
new	results	health
easy	safety	love
proven	yes	guarantee
free	sale	now
secrets	why	yes
fast	how	announcing

Colorful, informative window signs can lure in passersby

NEW LISTINGS

Caledonia Realty

800·555·HOME

Just Listed!
Contemporary 3-bedroom, 2-bath with double garage. Great location in a quiet cul-du-sac. Near stores and schools. Rare find in this most desirable neighborhood.
$225,00

Pastoral Setting, Urban Convenience
Newly remodeled with cathedral ceilings and a gourmet kitchen! Move-in condition. 2 bedrooms, 1.5 baths. Hot tub and formal garden. This one won't last long!
$300,000

conscious impression on your customer and your signs should awaken that memory. Working together, ads and signs make customers feel confident rather than confused. (Is this the same place that advertised in Sunday's paper?) Signs also trigger impulse sales, so it's a good idea to hang unique signs when you're announcing a sale or a new product arrival.

Posters

Posters are a versitile marketing tool. Poster-sized photos (with a discrete message, of course) always attract attention and can be used in windows or throughout the store. Posters are also great giveaway items. For example, give every kid a poster of the Matchbox cars your toy store sells or provide florist customers with a poster listing hints on keeping flowers fresh. Everyone likes to get something for nothing.

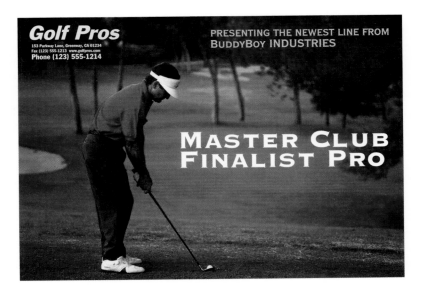

Posters can be used equally well for advertising and decoration

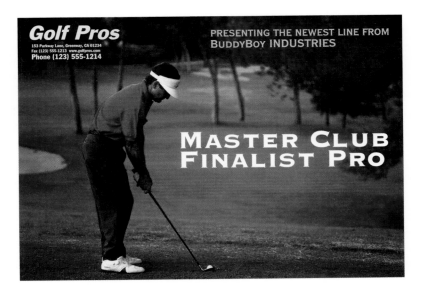

Golf Pros
153 Parkway Lane, Greenway, CA 01234
Fax (123) 555-1213 www.golfpros.com
Phone (123) 555-1214

PRESENTING THE NEWEST LINE FROM
BUDDYBOY INDUSTRIES

MASTER CLUB FINALIST PRO

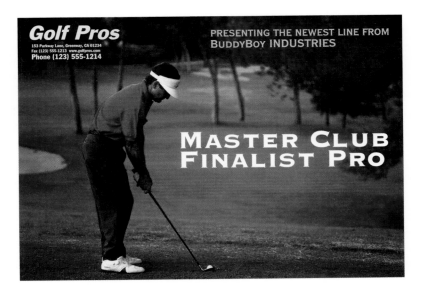

Signs

187

Posters are also effective when hung as decorations or used as freestanding inserts in newspapers or regional magazines. A word of warning: When you're sending posters as direct mail pieces, always use a mailing tube. If the poster can't be displayed once it's received, you've lost a lot of free publicity.

Banners

When you really want to get noticed, there's nothing like a banner strung across your building or running from the trees to your store. Banners are great for grand openings, remodelings, or sidewalk sales. If you can get other businesses to go in with you, you can even turn it into a neighborhood event. String a banner across the street, set up some tables, and you've got a street fair. And you don't need to be in retail to get something out of it. Banks can hand out piggy banks with their flyers or cleaners can give away coupons for special discounts. Restaurants can get into the act by serving samples and distributing

MARKETING TIPS

◆ Clear lettering is essential

◆ Make the message readable in 3 seconds

◆ Unite with others to hang a banner

◆ Create an impulse to buy

◆ Be sure advertisements and signs reinforce each other

Adding a photo to a bulletin board sign helps it stand out from the sea of words

take-out menus. Banners of this magnitude are best created by banner companies. You can find one in the ubiquitous Yellow Pages.

Bulletin board signs

For some guerrillas, bulletin board signs have proven to be a very effective advertising medium. A quick glance at a neighborhood bulletin board is likely to reveal 3 x 5 cards for gardeners, plumbers, typists, writers, baby-sitters, movers, accountants, music teachers, answering services, cleaning services, astrologists, and entertainers. You get the idea. If you're in a service business, bulletin board signs may be your ticket to paradise.

You won't have to look far to find a bulletin board. Take a field trip in your community and you'll see boards in libraries, laundromats, locker rooms, barbershops, day-care centers, and bookstores, to name just a few. Don't ignore offices either. They often have bulletin boards in lobbies, cafeterias,

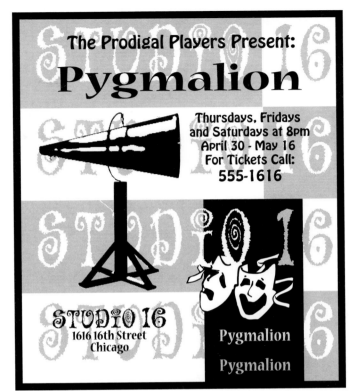

Black and white signs can be lively, attractive, and different enough to demand attention

hallways, and rest rooms. When you're out locating boards, take time to check out the competition. You can even call some of the companies and ask what kind of response they're getting from their small signs.

You can post bulletin board signs yourself or hire someone to do it for you. Doing it yourself is the cheapest way. If your business is growing, however, there's probably a more profitable way for you to spend your time. The proverbial high-school kid is another choice. For the best results, though, nothing compares with a professional posting service. Finding a posting service is as near as your trusty Yellow Pages.

Once the signs are posted, keep up your research. Ask customers where they saw your sign and you'll quickly find the best posting locations. Make sure you or your representative checks the signs frequently. It's also a good idea to change the sign periodically. Keep the same message but add a new twist to keep up browser interest.

Print terminology

Although it may never come up if you make your own signs and other marketing materials, you might be curious about how printers talk about type. In case you need it (or if you just want to impress your friends), here're some type terms for your edification:

- **baseline**—an imaginary horizontal line that all type characters in a line must touch.

- **font**—the complete assortment of type of one face and one size, including upper- and lowercase letters, punctuation, and numerals.

- **kerning**—subtracting space between certain combinations of type characters to tighten the fit and improve the readability and appearance.

- **leading**—the distance between type lines, measured in points from the baseline of one line of type to the baseline of the next line.

- **pica**—a unit of type measurement. One pica is approximately equal to one-sixth of an inch.

- **point**—a unit of type measurement. One point is approximately equal to one-seventy-second of an inch. Twelve points equal one pica.

- **rule**—line used for borders, boxes, and many other purposes, for example, to separate elements or columns.

- **sans serif**—letterforms without serifs and usually having a single thickness of line.

- **serif**—the ending strokes of characters; short cross lines at the end of main strokes.

- **type family**—all the variations of a specific typeface design. For example, Minion, Minion Black, Minion Black OsF, Minion Bold, Minion BoldItalic, Minion BoldItalicOsF, Minion Display, Minion Display Italic, Minion Expert, Minion Expert Black, Minion ItalicSC, and Minon Semibold are all one type family.

- **type size**—the size of the type usually measured in points.

- **typeface**—a particular style of type design including the full range of characters, in all sizes.

Correct a scanned photo

This scan of this photo came in too dark and in the wrong orientation. There are several ways you can fix such problems in PhotoDeluxe Business Edition. The easiest, and first ones to try, are those in the Get & Fix Photo > Touch Up and Get & Fix Photo > Repair guided activities. When you need more tools, you can explore those found in the Advanced section. Here are the tools used to fix this photo.

Designing the sign

Words are the most important element in a sign but you don't want to have too many of them. Most signs are read quickly, so keep the copy down to six words. Make the type as large as possible and make the headline the largest of all. You don't need to worry about punctuation; the only piece you might need is an exclamation point to add a sense of excitement. It's best to use light letters against a dark background or dark letters against a light background.

Using a photo or graphic is a good substitute for words. If you're going to do a lot of signs, a strong graphic is almost mandatory. Think of the power of the Marlboro Man or the Absolut bottle. To get the best results, find an easily identifiable symbol and then use it consistently. ■

Rotate Right

To rotate the photo so it's in the correct orientation

Trim

To trim off the black edges from the original scan

Photo Size

To make the photo the correct size for a window sign

Extensis IntelliFix

To lighten and color-correct the photo

These simple steps resulted in a photo that 's 100% better than the original

P-O-P displays

Seizing the moment

*A*dweek magazine reports that point-of-purchase materials account for up to 80% of many advertisers' budgets. The success of point-of-purchase (P-O-P) materials is credited to their ability to connect mass media marketing with the consumer *AT THE TIME OF PURCHASE*. Since research shows that 74% of all buying decisions are made at the place of purchase, the power of P-O-P becomes awesome.

Shelf-talkers are designed to extend into the aisle to catch the buyer's eye. This example uses the Shelf Talk 4 template in the Projects > Promote > Retail Displays guided activity.

Why P-O-P works

The theory behind P-O-P advertising is that people enter a store vaguely interested in buying a certain item, but they don't make up their mind until they're right there. Remember, people are not in your store by accident; they are serious about buying from you. P-O-P displays offer just the note of encouragement and motivation needed at the very moment of the sale.

Research confirms that retailers who use point-of-purchase displays generate more sales from on-site customers. In one study, 56% of convenience store managers said that P-O-P materials are extremely effective in increasing sales; 48% of supermarket managers agreed.

Point-of-purchase displays capitalize on the presence of the buyer by offering instant rewards and instant gratification. They can be used to invite customers to touch, taste, try out, or try on your offering. Think of them as unobtrusive, silent salespersons. They not only remind prospects that your product exists, they can also persuade a customer to buy your product over someone else's.

194

Daily and monthly specials are perfect material for table tents. This example uses the Tent 2 template in Projects > Promote > Retail Displays and is printed on the Avery Table Tent stock.

What's on P-O-P displays?

In addition to motivating and inviting, P-O-P displays are good places to list features and benefits, explain complex points, and compare your product with the competition. For example, gourmet groceries often list specific product ingredients, electronics stores list technical highlights, and music stores reprint reviews or give *Billboard* ratings.

There are also P-O-P displays that are designed to provide information rather than incite an instant sale. These could be the type of information brochures that you get from car sales representatives and computer retailers. Or the P-O-P may display performance charts or testimonials from satisfied customers.

Ads are meant to create desires, but P-O-P displays are meant to create impulse buys. For example, a customer may come in to buy dog food, but while they're there, you'd also like them to buy a leash, a doggie door, and a heated dog bed. Make your P-O-P materials as potent as possible. Ideally, P-O-P displays enlarge the size of a transaction and win new customers. The point is to move as

Color and clip art can turn an ordinary coupon into a mini work of art. This P-O-P was created using the coupon04 template in Projects > Promote > Coupons.

much merchandise or sell as many services as possible, right on the spot.

Don't overlook the tremendous opportunity to use P-O-P as containers for coupons, new product announcements, and sweepstakes and contest entries. No matter how good the economy is, people still want to save money, believe they're getting a special deal, and have the chance to get something for nothing.

Designing a P-O-P display

All P-O-P displays have two things in common: The message is extremely simple and they are blindingly bright.

While these interior signs can have more words than outdoor signs, the clearest message is still the best. Nothing words better than the old favorites, WIN!, FREE!, 20% OFF!, LIMITED TIME ONLY. This is not the place for subtlety.

PhotoDeluxe Business Edition has several templates to help you create visually powerful P-O-P displays. These templates are found in the Projects > Promote > Retail Display guided activity. There are templates for shelf-talkers (small cards that attach to shelves and project into the aisle), and table tents (folded two-sided cardboard signs

MARKETING TIPS

◆ Use traffic flow to determine P-O-P display placement

◆ Research competitors to see how they're using P-O-P displays

◆ Motivate, compel, and inform, but most importantly, SELL

◆ Offer something for nothing

◆ Go to any length to get your P-O-P materials displayed

Determining shelf life

When you're creating P-O-P displays, think about how long you want them to last. Your industry may favor self-shipping, disposable displays. Made of corrugated cardboard containers, these "dumps" as they are sometimes called, are meant to be disposed of once they're empty. Although easy to assemble, dumps don't do anything to establish your long-term presence in the store.

Permanent displays are more expensive but worth investigating if your product is going to stay in the store for some time. Prime users of permanent displays include cosmetics companies in department stores, manufacturers of golf clubs for pro shops, and even toothbrush manufacturers. The beauty of these displays is that they take on a life of their own and serve to make it easier to locate as well as buy the product. If you can convince retailers that they will enjoy increased profits as the result of your permanent display, they'll agree to put it in the store.

196

that stand on tables or counters). The templates for coupons are found in Projects > Promote > Coupons. There are specific Avery papers designed to print your table tents and coupons. For more information, see "Using Avery paper stock" in the Labels topic.

In addition to these templates, you can use P-O-P displays to distribute flyers, reprints of ads, and direct mail postcards. Or use a big display to help customers locate a product. Anything that gets the customer's attention and prompts them to fork over the cash is fair game.

When you're writing the copy and choosing graphics for a P-O-P display, put yourself in the place of the person at the moment of purchase. Does the message compel you to buy right now? Does the message give you the information you want? Put you in a buying mood? Give you so many reasons to buy that you can hardly resist? Good P-O-P materials do.

To keep the message of your advertisements going, tie the P-O-P design into the style and copy of your ad campaign. Finish the message your ad begins by including some of the same words or a trademark graphic or slogan. Smart guerrillas know that in effective advertising campaigns, all the elements work together.

Taking what's given

If you're a retailer, you may not have to design your own P-O-P displays. Many manufacturers offer free point-of-purchase materials with their products. Whenever you're ordering a product, particularly when it's a new product, ask if any signs, brochures, display racks, window banners, counter cards, or coupons come as part of the marketing package.

If you're a manufacturer, be sure that your retailers are using the materials you're giving them. The best-designed P-O-P display does nothing to increase sales if it remains unpacked in the back room. You need to have your salespeople and distributors take the initiative and set up the displays themselves. If necessary, roll up your sleeves and do it yourself. The increase in sales that comes from using P-O-P materials is worth every bit of effort needed to convince retailers to set up the displays. ■

Add color to black-and-white clip art

Sometimes the perfect piece of clip art is only available in black and white when you need color to fit your design. In PhotoDeluxe Business Edition, adding color to your black-and-white clip art is a cinch.

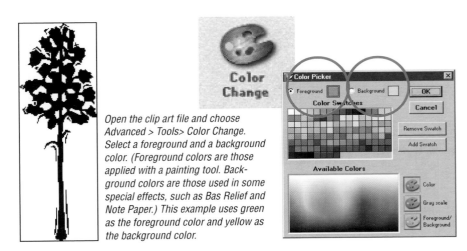

Open the clip art file and choose Advanced > Tools> Color Change. Select a foreground and a background color. (Foreground colors are those applied with a painting tool. Background colors are those used in some special effects, such as Bas Relief and Note Paper.) This example uses green as the foreground color and yellow as the background color.

Choose Advanced > Effects > Special Effects > Elegant > Note Paper. The dialog box shows you a preview of the colorization. Don't hesitate to cancel and go back to Color Change to select new colors if you don't like the effect the first time around.

Labels

Delivering with style

U ntil now, return address labels have not exactly been a bastion of creative marketing. Letters and packages usually went out with white, weirdly spaced return labels or handwritten return addresses. With PhotoDeluxe Business Edition, however, you can carry your business identity right through to your return labels. And to your shipping, video, CD-ROM, cassette, and diskette labels too.

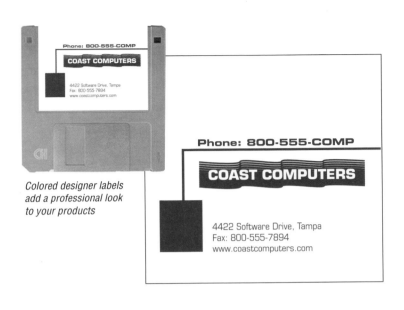

*Colored designer labels
add a professional look
to your products*

*Using your logo on labels
reinforces your market
identity. This example uses
the video4 template in the
Projects > Forms > Labels
guided activity.*

Why create labels?

While you'll probably stick to your
printed envelopes for letters, there are
times when you need printed return
address labels. For example, you'll want
company labels when you send out
postcards, flyers, self-seal mailers, packages, and calenders. Company labels are
also a handy way to provide name tags,
identify property, decorate cubicles, personalize office equipment, and label the
backs of unsuspecting co-workers.

DESIGN TIPS

◆ Decide if you want
the label to blend in
or contrast with the
envelope or
packaging

◆ Verify that the
design conforms
with shipping and
postal regulations

◆ Don't make the
label too busy

Using Avery paper stock

You follow the same steps to use Avery paper stock whether you're printing business cards, invitations, cards, calendars, retail displays, or labels. To get to the Avery selection of papers, you use the Multiple on a Page guided activity.

To use an Avery stock:

1. Choose Send & Save> To Printer > Multiple on a Page.

2. Click Type and then click Choose Type.

3. In the Choose Paper Type dialog box, choose Avery. One of the Avery products will be chosen by default.

   The numbers in front of the paper types in the dialog box refer to the ordering number (or SKU) for the Avery paper. Use this number to order the right stock.

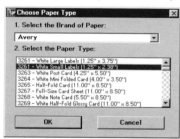

4. To change the paper type, click on a new type.

5. Click OK.

6. Click Print and then Print Multiple.

   The Print Multiple dialog box shows you a preview of the printed page. You can change the number of copies or the paper type.

7. Click Print. After printing is completed, click Done to leave the guided activity.

For more information on Avery stock, choose Avery in the online help index. To see a listing of the templates and the default Avery papers, click the U.S. Avery paper stock or International Avery paper stock topics in online help.

You can even visit the Avery online catalog directly from PhotoDeluxe Business Edition. To get to the Avery home page, click Internet > Avery > Avery.

742 Willow Street, Pacifica, CA 01234

Exotic Floral Designs
The beauty of the islands and the smell of the sea…

How many people do you suppose see your logo in the course of handling your mailings?

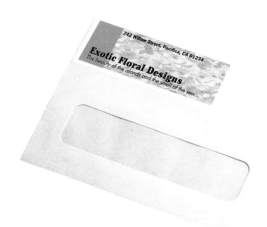

Beyond address and shipping labels, PhotoDeluxe Business Edition provides templates for just about any kind of label you might need. Many companies, for example, fail to take advantage of diskette labels, which not only identify the diskette contents but provide a very visible marketing opportunity. This same sense of professionalism is apparent when you create custom labels for video brochures and annual reports, marketing or instructional CD-ROMs, or audio cassettes of interviews, conferences, or presentations.

Producing a label

In most cases, you'll probably use the Projects > Forms > Labels guided activity to make a return or shipping label that matches your stationery. If you want to be creative, you might add a teaser or tag line to labels for direct mail pieces. You can even include instructions on labels, for example, "HANDLE WITH CARE." For a really unique shipping label, put a photo of the contents on the label and include a message. For example, include a photo of the book jacket on a shipping label for mail-ordered books or a picture of the computer on the packing carton with the message, "Here's Your New Computer!"

Downloading Avery guided activities

Avery also supplies some guided activities to use with their products. These activities let you print sheets of labels.

To download an Avery guided activity:

1. Click Internet> Avery> Guided Activities.

2. Follow the steps to download the template you want to use.

3. Choose File> Open File.

4. Move to the location where you've installed PhotoDeluxe Business Edition.

5. Open the Program Files folder.

6. Open the PhotoDeluxe BE 1.0 folder.

7. Open the PD Gallry folder.

8. Open the Samples folder.

9. Choose the template you want to use and click Open.

The template opens as an unnamed PhotoDeluxe Business Edition file.

The Avery connection

Many of the PhotoDeluxe Business Edition templates are presized to be printed on paper types supplied by Avery. The Avery stock includes paper for business cards, note cards, postcards, table tents, and self-seal mailers. But, by far, the largest selection of output choices are available for labels.

You can choose from several types and sizes of address labels, shipping labels, video cassette spine and face labels,

Create all kinds of labels

Labels come in all sizes and colors (you can even get transparent labels). Try using labels for personal statements, tag lines, warnings, advice, information, and decoration.

FREE OFFER ENCLOSED

Clear shipping label used for a teaser

Floppy disk label used for a warning

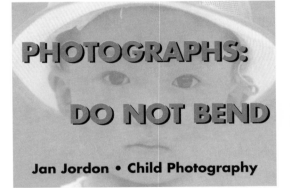

PHOTOGRAPHS:

DO NOT BEND

Jan Jordon • Child Photography

name badge kits, diskettes labels, Re-move 'Em labels, ink jet labels, and glossy photo-quality labels.

When you use a template to produce a label, one of the Avery papers is chosen by default. You can use the suggested paper stock or choose a different type of paper. If you choose a paper that's smaller than the template size, the tem-plate contents are reduced to fit the paper. If you choose a paper that's big-ger than your template, the template contents are centered on the page. ■

WILDLIFE
Rescue
Help Us Help Them!

Address labels used as stickers

Valley Vets
means healthy pets
800-555-0187

All It Takes Is A Little Planning **Wonderful Weddings**

Video spine label

T-shirts

Wearing your advertising

Being the hip, slick, and cool guerrilla that you are, you know that T-shirts are the clothing of choice for most generations on most occasions. Everyone from your grandmother to your kid wears T-shirts. Okay, when it's cold they might wear sweatshirts. Since it's a shame to waste all that potential advertising space, it's definitely time your company got a T-shirt.

Company T-shirts are a great way to promote your business

Company T-shirts

No matter what type of business you're in, it can't hurt to have a T-shirt. Your regular, run-of-the-mill T-shirt probably will have only your logo and company name. It could also include your tag line or location. With a little more thought, and if it's appropriate, you might also put a saying or slogan on the shirt. Or start a teaser on the front (Is your kitchen bugging you?) and continue with the punch line on the back (call Primo Terminators Today!).

These standard T-shirts are the ones you sell in your restaurant, fitness center, or store. Some companies have their employees wear T-shirts to help customers identify salespersons. In any case, company T-shirts don't need to be anything fancy.

DESIGN TIPS

◆ Consider if the design will be printed on one or several colors

◆ Include the phone number

◆ Use a design that enlarges and reduces well

◆ Use graphics from other advertising

Create personalized T-shirts as gifts for valued customers. This T-shirt uses the Tshirt5 template in the Projects > Promote > T-Shirt Transfer guided activity.

petsitters, inc.

Special-event T-shirts

Another great occasion to print T-shirts is when you're participating in or sponsoring a special event such as a race, a benefit concert, a street fair, or a summer camp. The shirts can be worn by participants in the event (BF Construction..In the Running for Your Business) or they can advertise your sponsorship (Valley Vet's 3rd Annual Low-Cost Vaccination Clinic). Making T-shirts with PhotoDeluxe Business Edi-

tion is as easy as ironing on a transfer sheet. This means you can even offer T-shirts as a unique personalized gift (Wonderful Weddings Congratulates Meg and Michael, June 7, 1999).

Contest and premium T-shirts

For maximum advertising effect, you can create T-shirts that proclaim a contest or commemorate a business milestone. For example, you could give a T-shirt away to everyone who returns a coupon to your store or fills out a customer ques-

Bay Area 10K Run

Sponsered by
WILDLIFE
Rescue

Help Us Help Them!
800-WILD

Sponsoring a special event is a great way to advertise your business as well as your commitment to the community

Sponsorship

If you're a business that has a lot of public contact, you might consider sponsoring an annual or ongoing community event. Sponsorship works well because you can sell a lot of tickets and generate lots of enthusiasm in your daily interactions with customers. Plus, your T-shirt will constantly be in the attention spotlight. Here're just a few sponsorship ideas:

- adopt a local soccer, baseball, or basketball team
- stage a charity sports event that pits your employees against local firefighters
- organize a running or walking race to raise money for a cause or local charity
- designate your location as a drop off center for Thanksgiving food or Christmas gifts for the homeless
- support your local police department's anti-drug campaign (such as DARE)
- present a lecture series on a subject of interest to your customers

MARKETING TIPS

◆ Buy in bulk to save money

◆ Require a trip to your place of business to pick up the T-shirt

◆ Use T-shirts to cross-promote with another guerrilla

◆ Remember brand awareness and actual sales are different things

tionnaire. You might also give away T-shirts to celebrate your grand opening, your 20th anniversary, or your first million in revenue. Computer companies are infamous for their project T-shirts and radio stations frequently give away T-shirts to call-in winners. Commemorative T-shirts should come in limited numbers so that they're valued as something unique and special.

Creating and printing your T-shirt

To use the PhotoDeluxe Business Edition T-shirt templates, choose Projects> Promote> T-Shirt Transfer. To print the T-shirt, you'll need to buy transfer paper sheets from your regular computer supply company. To print, choose Send & Save> To Printer> Print T-shirt. ■

Get involved with your community

Every enterprising guerrilla knows the truth of the old adage—you can do well by doing good. Become involved in your community because it's the right thing to do. Enjoy customer's loyalty and increased sales because you're doing what your heart believes. People like doing business with companies that demonstrate concern for more than simply maximizing their profits.

The key to community involvement is finding a group that overlaps with your target market. It just makes sense to provide a service to groups or organizations that will also bring you new customers or prospects. You can start by donating your time to a neighborhood charity. Or, you can provide discounts to local non-profit groups. And there is no organization in existence that will turn down a cash donation.

The free publicity and positive word-of-mouth advertising that results from your sincere involvement will more than make up for any time, goods, discounts, or money that you contribute.

To find out where you might be of service, check with your local business associations or just take a look around. You can develop community understanding and goodwill by doing any of the following:

- serve food at a local homeless shelter

- allow local artists to exhibit in your place of business

- lend tools or give supplies for a "fix up a home" day

- donate your parking lot for a benefit car wash

- provide space in your newsletter for discussion of local environmental and political issues

- offer the school new computer equipment for every $50,000 in receipts from your store

- establish a local scholarship fund

- contribute merchandise that can be auctioned off or presented as raffle prizes

Create a color vignette

One attractive, effective way to blend photos with a background is to use a vignette. A soft-edged vignette allows your design to break away from the rectangle format of most photos.

Open the photo. This example uses the eaglebig photo from the Get & Fix Photo > Get Photo > Sample Photos > Nature gallery.

Use the Oval tool in the Selections palette to select the area you want to include in the vignette

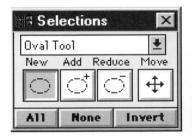

Choose the Advanced > Effects > Feather tool

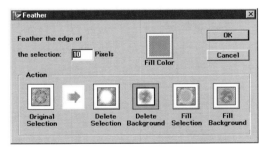

This example uses a Feather value of 10 and the Delete Background action

Bay Area
10K Run

sponsored by
WILDLIFE
Rescue

Help Us Help Them!
800-WILD

Feathering the edges helps the photo merge into the white background of the T-shirt without a distracting border

In-person Marketing *211*

Presentations

Persuading
with
graphics

Adding graphics can go a long way toward jazzing up a presentation. You can use any of the PhotoDeluxe Business Edition tools to prepare graphics and photos for your presentation. When you're ready to create slides, put slides in order, and add transitions, you'll want to use a presentation package such as Adobe Persuasion.

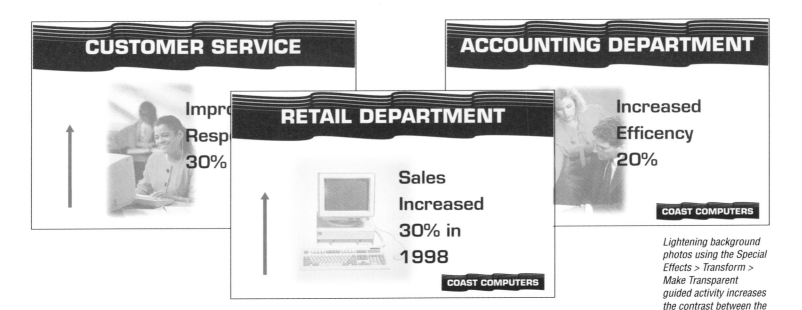

Lightening background photos using the Special Effects > Transform > Make Transparent guided activity increases the contrast between the text and the photo

How graphics can help

Without a doubt, one of the most frequent complaints about presentations is that there is too much text. This might be too much text on a slide, too much text in a bulleted item, text that's too small to read, or just too many text slides in a row. One good use for graphics in slides is to provide a pleasant but non-obtrusive background for text. Even this simple trick helps break up boring blocks of black text.

Using a consistent graphic on your slides, even if it's just your company name and logo, can help keep your presentation flowing. Or try using a repeating photo in one corner of the slide that changes when you move into a new topic or subject area.

Graphics can also be used as replacements for text. Instead of describing a product, show a picture of it. Instead of listing benefits, show the product in use. Have different departments use a unique graphic slide to introduce their sections. The more detail you need to go into, the more graphics you need. Add photos of your employees, of satisfied customers, or of your new offices.

Don't make the same mistake with graphics that's made with text. Use photos and graphics in moderation and for a specific purpose. The point is to communicate information to the audience. Make sure the slide design and use of graphics add to the communication, not the confusion.

Presentation tips

When deciding how to use graphics in your presentation, work in conjunction with your presentation outline and purpose. Most presentations fall into three different sections that can be delineated by graphics or color:

The **introduction** is where you define the problem, state your goal or purpose, and cite what you want to accomplish or what actions you want to take place at the end of the presentation.

The **rationale** section presents the solution and lays out your plan of attack. It provides supporting facts and figures and discusses some of the implications of the research or data.

The **reemphasis** sums up the main points and asks for the order or approval needed to move forward. Don't make the mistake of giving an open-ended presentation. Know the result you want and then go for it!

Cindy Cane has been with Sunflower Day Care Center for 5 years. You can also find Cindy jogging and hiking in her free time.

Lisa Davis has been with Sunflower Day Care Center for 3 years. Lisa is currently continuing her education in child development.

Everyone likes to see themselves up on the big screen. These employee photos are framed using templates from the Projects > Presentations > Frames guided activity.

Using color to unify

Putting a color border or frame around a photo can provide a nice contrast to bulleted lines of text. You can also use simple color boxes or lines to divide the slide into graphic and text areas. Reinforce a theme by tinting all photos in a specific section the same color.

It's best to use a limited number of colors in the slide. Too many colors tend to draw attention away from the text and provide conflicting centers of attention. Make sure the colors in the background complement the text and always use contrasting texts and backgrounds. Patterned backgrounds also work well as long as they don't interfere with the text.

Using a few key words can make a slide more effective

Dressing up text

Your can add interest to your slide headlines by using subtle special effects, such as shadow text or reverse type. In general, keep away from fancy type and effects for the slide contents; it makes smaller text both distracting and difficult to read.

Keep most of your text in the horizontal plane although you can put easily identifiable text, such as your company name or section titles, along the vertical edge of a slide.

Handing out copies

If you'll be distributing printed copies of your presentation, keep this in mind when you're deciding on graphics and colors. Background graphics can take a long time to print and may obscure text when printed—especially if they're printed on low-resolution or grayscale printers. Some contrasting colors do not convert well into print.

If your presentation uses a lot of graphics, gradients, and special text effects, it's a good idea to produce a simplified version for print. For example, you can eliminate background graphics, substi-

The secret of combining typefaces

While your goal should be to use text that's easy to read, this does not have to translate into boring. When you use only one type family, without varying the style, size, or weight very much, the resulting piece appears sedate. This may be fine if you're going for a formal look, but otherwise it can be incredibly dull.

If you decide to venture into the world of two or more typefaces, make sure that the type families are not very similar. Contrary to what you may think, similar typefaces are more confusing than very distinct ones. You want to emphasize the contrast between the two typefaces to get the most appealing effect. The more contrast, the clearer the message.

There are six characteristics to keep in mind when you're picking contrasting type: size, weight (thickness), structure, form (shape), direction, and color. Try out different combinations by varying these elements one at a time. Remember, don't try too many varieties at once and keep the typefaces very distinct. You'll be surprised at the exciting and professional looks you can create.

DESIGN TIPS

◆ Create subtle background graphics

◆ Use color to unify or distinguish sections or topics

◆ Keep each slide to 12 words or less

◆ Combine contrasting typefaces

◆ Make sure graphics contribute to the communication

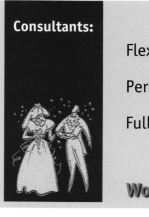

Conservative colors give this presentation an elegant, formal look. The shadow text in this slide was created using the Projects > Presentations > Drop Shadows guided activity.

tute clip art for photos, or eliminate multiple colors for text.

When you're doing a presentation as part of a sales call or trade show exhibit, don't miss the opportunity to hand out your other marketing materials as well: business cards, newsletters, brochures, flyers, product sheets, posters, and inserts. "Repurpose" is the guerrilla's mantra. ■

Use special effects on text

To use special effects on text, you must first turn the text into a graphic. For complete instructions for creating a graphic from text, see the "Change text into a graphic" how to in Reminders. In this example, the Perspective effect was used on text to create an attention-grabbing headline.

Reduce Home Remodeling Costs

Opening the saved JPEG file shows that the text is now on Layer O and ready to be manipulated

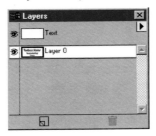

The Advanced > Size > Perspective tool was used to create the distortion

The photo to be used as the background was dragged into the text file resulting in a new layer (Layer 1). This layer was moved below the layer containing the text graphic.

When you create a JPEG file, the text automatically appears on a white background. This background is dragged along with the text.

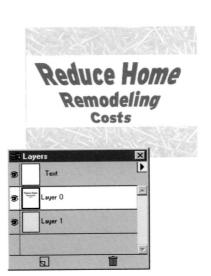

To delete the white background, the white areas were selected using the Color Wand selection tool. (Be sure to select areas inside the letters as well as the background.) The Delete key was used to remove the selected areas.

Trade shows

Making a public spectacle of yourself

Exhibiting at a trade show is an increasingly important part of many guerrilla marketing programs. According to American Business Press research, trade shows rank as the "most useful" marketing media to 67.7% of those polled. The obvious reason—trade shows are the best way to reach the largest number of real prospects at one time in one place. Enough said.

Send out invitations to trade show events early enough for prospects to plan their schedules

Are trade shows for you?

In general, trade shows work best for people who sell products rather than services. To see if trade shows might be a good strategy for your business, call your local trade association and find out the current trade show schedule. Go to at least one show as a visitor. Is your competition exhibiting at the show? Are they getting a good response? You might even ask a few exhibitors about their trade show experience. You'll soon get a feel if this might be a profitable venue for your company.

While you're at the show, take note of things that you like, things that attract your attention, and things that annoy you. Sketch the booths and displays that make you feel welcome and those that turn you off. Notice how signs are hung, how traffic flow is managed, and how deals are made (or not made!). If you see a booth you really admire, ask the exhibitor who designed it. This information will be invaluable if you later decide you want to participate in a trade show.

Flyers handed out at the front doors or on the floor pull people to your booth, especially if you offer a chance to win something

What trade shows can do

For some entrepreneurs, the contacts made at trade shows are enough to generate a year's worth of orders. In addition to actual selling, trade shows are the perfect place to establish long-term relationships with prospects and clients. In these times of teleconferencing, faxes, and email, the personal contacts established at trade shows can go a long way toward cementing deals with repeat and new customers.

Who attends trade shows

Aside from prowling guerrillas who are just there to check it out, most trade show visitors (34%) are top or middle managers. This is great news because these folks are the decision makers, and most of them are there to buy. Approximately 21% are in sales and marketing, 20% are in engineering or research, and 12% are production or operation supervisors.

Most visitors stop at about 20 booths per show and spend about 15 minutes at each booth. Keep this in mind when you're planning your demonstration or sales spiel. With so much input and so little time, you need to do your best to make an impression on these busy, information-overloaded, multimedia-blitzed attendees.

Doing your homework

The work of exhibiting at a trade show begins well before the actual show opens. You first job is to pick the right show. There are hundreds of local and national shows, so you need to research which show or shows will work best for you. Ask yourself the relevant questions: Who will be attending? How much does it cost? How much time will it take away from running the business? Who are the other exhibitors? Does the show have a reputation for quality?

Once you decide on a show, figure out your main goal in putting up an exhibit. Do you want to penetrate your existing market or are you going for a new market? In other words, is the plan to make sales or collect leads? Your goal will de-

Bring plenty of brochures to hand out

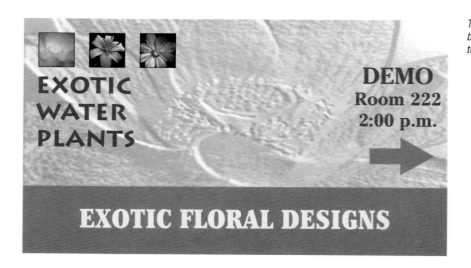

Trade show signs should be big, bright, and easy to read from a distance

fine many of the exhibit elements, from layout and design to premium giveaways.

Pre-show advertising

Trade shows take a lot of planning. You can't just decide to exhibit and then show up and wait for the crowds. Crowds is the key word here—there will be plenty of people wandering up and down miles and miles of aisles. You need to make sure they stop at your booth.

Send invitations to all your prospects and invite them to pick up something free at your booth. Better yet, make your invitation an entry form for a contest that people can enter by visiting your booth. Provide them with show schedules and a photo and map to your booth. Make it as compelling and easy as possible to find you.

Check with the show management to see if you can offer a seminar or host a hospitality suite, party, or early-morning breakfast. You'll want to include this information and possibly tickets or passes in your invitations.

Designing the booth

If it's worth spending the fee to exhibit at the show, it's probably worth getting a professional designer to create, set up, and dismantle your booth. Such people are listed in the Yellow Pages under "Display Designers and Producers" or a similar category. This is their job and they know how to do it.

Tickets for drawings, parties, and demonstrations are essential. This ticket (template ticket01) was created using the Projects > Cards > Tickets guided activity.

ADMIT ONE

Exotic Floral Designs Show

May 15, 1999

Sunset Auditorium
20 Magnolia Lane
Pacifica, CA

Your job is to make sure that the exhibit reflects your marketing identity and current advertising campaign. If it's appropriate, plan a hands-on demonstration or set out something people can handle. Decide who is going to staff your booth. Early on, contact the companies that can supply you with that all-important giveaway item. Make sure you allow yourself enough time to make carefully researched choices.

Basic advertising strategy also applies to trade show booths. Keep the message focused, short, and simple. A few large pictures and a company sign might be all you need. If you use display signs, make sure they broadcast benefits and the message that Your Problems Are Solved Here.

Once you're there

One of the most important elements in a show's profitability or loss is the quality of the people working the booth. These can be your own employees or hired professionals. Above all, the staff must be personable and knowledgeable about your company and product. They must understand how to close sales, have the power to conclude deals, and know when a lead is hot, warm, or stone cold. With so many people stopping by, your staff must be polite, yet smart—they can't afford to waste time with people not ready to buy. 20% of visitors account for 80% of trade show sales, and your sales reps need to concentrate on this critical 20%. Plan your

Keep the booth message focused, short, and simple.

Press releases and publicity

Press releases and publicity stories are not just for trade shows or limited to large, multinational companies. You can attract a lot of attention for your small business by writing and distributing publicity pieces. It's easier to get press exposure if you follow a few simple guidelines:

- Make a list of the publications you think might be interested in your product and do some research. Find out what kinds of stories they print and who makes up their audiences.

- Call the editorial office and find out if there are any special requirements. Request the name of the person who should receive the materials or the name of a writer who might be interested in covering your story.

- Write a personal cover letter that reveals your knowledge of the publication.

- Make sure the press release or story is newsworthy. Emphasize why you're releasing it now and highlight what's interesting about your product or service.

- Write the story clearly and without hype.

- Follow up with a phone call to make sure the story was received.

schedule carefully so that there is *always* a knowledgeable person at the booth.

Be prepared to hand out brochures to serious prospects and have a ready supply of business cards. You might also want someone to circulate through the crowd handing out flyers, ads, contest announcements, or free passes to demonstrations.

Keep your actual sales pitch or demonstration short and to the point. If you only have 15 minutes of a prospect's time, don't spend more than 10 minutes on your presentation. You want to leave plenty of time for questions and comments. If more time is required to cement a deal, have a quiet area in your booth and chairs where sales negotiations can take place. It is never a good strategy to say, "Let me take your name and number and I'll have someone call you." Mostly likely, that prospect will walk right over to a competitor's booth and buy from them.

Supply the press room with plenty of press releases. Try to attend or have a representative at all the relevant press conferences. It's a good idea to get a copy of the list of press attendees so you can spot them as they wander by your booth.

Following up

If your goal is to generate leads, the most important part of the trade show takes place after it's over. This is when you send your follow-up mailings or make your follow-up phone calls. As a rule, follow up with prospects within 10 days of the show. Send every person a personal letter along with a brochure. You may need to send out as many as three or four letters, but in the end the results of trade shows can be well worth the time and money. ■

Duplicate parts of photos

Duplicating part of a photo in another location is fun and easy when you use the Clone tool.

To duplicate a photo between files, open both files. One file contains the photo area you want to duplicate and the other is the photo you're copying into. Make sure the photo you're copying from is selected (click anywhere in the photo to select it).

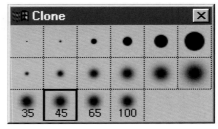

Choose Advanced > Tools > Clone and choose a brush size. This example uses a large soft-edged brush.

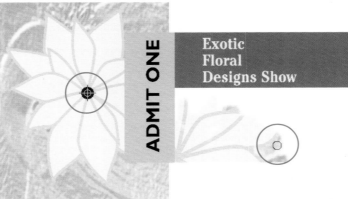

Move the target-shaped starting point to the area you want to duplicate. Click in the file you're copying to and begin painting. If you need to, you can change brush sizes as you go along.

You can move the target and then return to painting as many times as necessary. In this example, the image was painted two times with the cloned areas in the new file overlapping each other.

Portfolios

Displaying
your wares

When you hear "portfolio," does your mind immediately jump to artists dressed in black or the latest stock market quotes? Maybe so, but in most businesses, portfolios are more functional items. Depending on what you do, your portfolio might contain designs, photographs, reviews, testimonials, product descriptions, sample policies, or price lists. When you need to create pages to go in albums or notebooks, PhotoDeluxe Business Edition has the templates to help you.

Photo albums of other patients provide entertaining waiting-room reading. This page was created using the tprodsht2 template in the Projects > Cards > Album Page guided acitivity.

Creating a portfolio

The layout of the items in your portfolio depends a great deal on what you're displaying. If this is a notebook of product sheets or price lists, you'll want to have your information organized for quick access. You may use color codes or tabs to separate sections or groups. The idea behind this kind of portfolio is to be able to answer specific questions quickly.

If you're a sales rep, your portfolio may contain a presentation or guidelines for a demonstration. In this case, the portfolio is meant to support your delivery and should contain easy-to-read cheat sheets. Or you may use the portfolio to show products or services during a sales call. In either case, the portfolio should contain pages that are simple and easy to read, by both you and the customer.

Portfolios that highlight individual work are more like graphic resumes. Here the page probably contain lots of photographs or drawings and text is kept to a minimum. If you use a portfolio to document your skills, it will probably be laid out in chronological order or according to specific projects. This type of portfo-

Gathering testimonials

The primary reason people don't buy from you is that you haven't earned their trust. One of the fastest ways to build trust is to provide prospects with testimonials. The most frightening part of testimonials is asking for them. While you need to be open (and even eager) to hear feedback from customers, you're still human. The thought of asking your clients to comment on your product or services may seem like an invitation to be inundated with complaints. If you can manage to put your insecurity on hold for just a few minutes, you'll probably be pleasantly surprised by the results.

The best tactic is to ask for testimonials directly. If you can't quite bring yourself to do this, try sending a survey to your customers. Ask a few simple questions about the quality of your product and the convenience of buying from you. Then invite customers to go one step further. For example, add "Please consider enclosing a personal letter that we can show to prospective customers to let them know how you feel about doing business with us." Always ask for letters from new customers. Many of them will be flattered to contribute to your testimonial collection.

Testimonials don't need to be complete letters. Just a few lines or a brief paragraph can pinpoint the essence of what's different and better about your company. Just be sure you check with a customer before using an abridged version of their comments.

The best testimonials clearly state the customer's problem, along with the real solution provided by your company. Encourage your customers to be as specific as possible. Words like "good" and "fine" are okay, but real facts (We increased our profits 65% in four months thanks to your service) or personal statements (My body feels 10 years younger since I started working with my personal trainer at "Get a Life!") are more potent. Make sure customers include their full names, addresses, and titles. Comments from M. Ryan, Illinois, don't carry as much weight as comments from Penelope Graham, President, Kangaroo Curriculums, 39 State Street, Southbrook, Illinois.

Life Insurance Specialist

Westwood Insurance

The Keller's

With so many changes going on in our lives—moving to a new house, children in new schools, new employment opportunities—we needed some solid advice and help in reviewing our insurance needs. Mary was always there when we called and eager to help us choose correctly and save money. We couldn't be more satisfied!

Karen and Bill Williams

As a single mom buying my first house, I knew I needed to check out mortgage and life insurance. Mary took the time to listen to my situation and devised a custom-designed package that met all my needs. I look forward to working with Mary for a long, long, time.

REPRESENTED BY MARY SMITH

174 Broadway Street • Jonesville, Pennsylvania 01234
phone (123) 555 1212 • fax (123) 555-1213 • www.westwood.com

Testimonials accompanied by photos of satisfied customers build immediate trust between you and potential buyers. This sheet uses template prodsht1.

DESIGN TIPS

◆ Consider laminating pages that are handled frequently

◆ Break up copy with photos

◆ Don't put too much on a singe sheet

◆ Imprint your logo on the outside of the portfolio or notebook

lio is meant to be viewed by a client who will be hiring you or your firm. In some cases, you may not even be present, so this type of portfolio must represent your company's quality and integrity for you.

Photo pages

You might use the templates in the Projects> Cards> Album Page guided activity inside your company as well. For example, you can create an employee photo album or add photos to individual employee biographies. Include photos of facilities under construction, company picnics, or special celebrations and then store them in the company archives. Some doctors, such as veterinarians or obstetricians, put together albums of their patients and display them in their waiting rooms.

Catalogs

If your product line lends itself to visual representation, you can use the product sheet templates in the Album Page activity to create simple catalogs. It's easy to modify the tem-

Photos of completed
projects increase the
impact of portfolio pages

Testimonial collections

The power of testimonials is legend—in brochures, newsletters, printed advertisements, direct mail campaigns, and flyers. No matter how small or large a purchase the customer is considering, they are always reassured when a prior buyer recounts how wonderful, practical, efficient, beneficial, or indispensable the product is.

As a guerrilla marketer, you should use testimonials whenever and wherever you can. Consider putting together a notebook of testimonials and letters of recommendation from your customers. Testimonials from real people, on real letterhead, is one of the fastest ways to generate confidence in your product or service. Potential customers, even the cynical ones, know that you can't buy

plates if you want to include a larger picture and more text on each page. These types of catalogs are often displayed on the floors of furniture, flooring, carpeting, and building supply stores for customers to browse through as they think through their ideas for redecorating or remodeling.

Create a texture

Textures, especially when they relate to your business, can provide an appealing background or border for portfolio pages. A construction company, for example, might use a grid texture reminiscent of drafting paper.

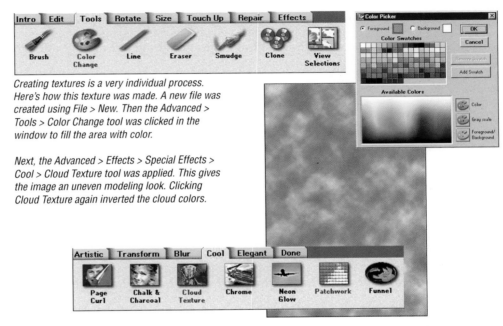

Creating textures is a very individual process. Here's how this texture was made. A new file was created using File > New. Then the Advanced > Tools > Color Change tool was clicked in the window to fill the area with color.

Next, the Advanced > Effects > Special Effects > Cool > Cloud Texture tool was applied. This gives the image an uneven modeling look. Clicking Cloud Texture again inverted the cloud colors.

praise at any price. Seeing page after page of glowing affidavits creates an overwhelming impact. Add smiling photos of your satisfied customers and the effect is magnified exponentially.

Carrying other marketing pieces

When choosing a portfolio case or cover, keep in mind what else you might like to have handy during a sales call or interview. Some portfolios contain pockets and enclosures for business cards, handouts, or extra copies of pages. You might also want to include brochures, flyers, or complimentary slips inside the case. Having all of these items in your portfolio can help you appear more polished and professional when you give your presentation or go out on a sales call. ■

As a finishing touch, the grid pattern was added using the Advanced > Effects > Special Effects > Cool > Patchwork tool. This texture is used as the border on the album page shown on the opposite page.

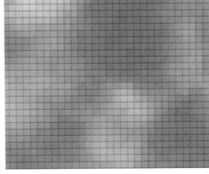

232

One-time Specials *233*

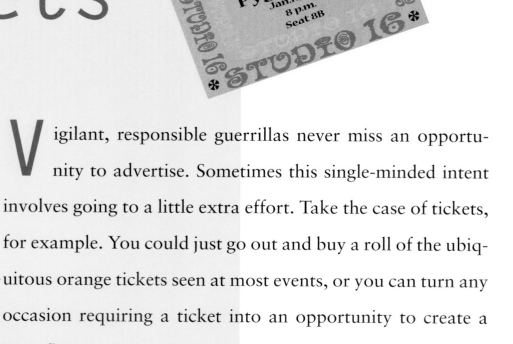

Tickets

Advertising for special events

Vigilant, responsible guerrillas never miss an opportunity to advertise. Sometimes this single-minded intent involves going to a little extra effort. Take the case of tickets, for example. You could just go out and buy a roll of the ubiquitous orange tickets seen at most events, or you can turn any occasion requiring a ticket into an opportunity to create a mini-flyer.

Frequent buyer cards encourage repeat business

Tickets for what?

You can issue tickets to almost every event, whether it's private or public, free or for a fee, required or optional.

First, there are tickets that allow entry. Somehow, when people have a ticket, they feel important and special. So while your main purpose for printing tickets may be to limit the number of participants, it will also strengthen relationships with customers. Think about the possibilities of customizing tickets for trade shows, exhibits, speeches, conferences, seminars, performances, festivals, benefits, lectures, openings, or parties.

You can also issue tickets that existing or potential customers can use to redeem gifts or discounts, enter a raffle or contest, or attend a school or community event that you're sponsoring. Make the tickets a little larger and you can leave room for names, addresses, and phone numbers. Then use this information to build your customer database.

What goes on the ticket?

Since you don't have much room, the key elements on the ticket should be the

DESIGN TIPS

◆ Don't forget to include the day of the week and the time

◆ Highlight your name and logo

◆ Print on glossy card stock to create a more durable ticket

◆ Include numbers to identify prize winners or number of purchases

Two companies joined together to sponsor this event. Both can add the ticket buyers to their customer databases.

event name, the time, the place, and the seat or room location. You'll also want to be sure that your name and logo appear prominently. Number the tickets if you're trying to track how many have been given out or if you're including door prizes or other gifts. The PhotoDeluxe Business Edition ticket templates are in the Projects > Cards > Tickets guided activity. All the templates include space for a photo as well as text. You might want to add a picture of the product or service you're featuring, announce speakers or special guests by name, add a fun or intriguing graphic,

or include a photo of your location. For an even fancier look, add a frame or special-effect border.

Frequent buyer cards

One special type of ticket that's becoming very popular is the frequent buyer card. These cards provide for discounts on future purchases once a number of products have been purchased or a specific dollar amount has been reached. Frequent buyer cards usually have an area that can be easily stamped or punched out to track the buyer's purchases. They are popular at fast-food restaurants, music and book stores,

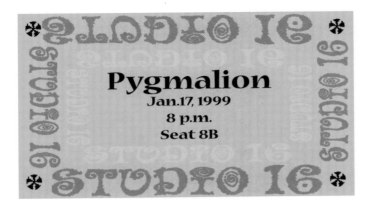

Theater tickets are often kept as mementos, which translates into free advertising for you

Pygmalion
Jan.17, 1999
8 p.m.
Seat 8B

beauty-supply stores, movies, and clothing stores. Besides providing incentive for repeat customers, frequent buyer cards also help you identify the 20% of your customer base that accounts for 50% to 80% of your sales. You want to get to know these people by name and single them out for special treatment by you and your staff.

Distributing tickets

How you get the tickets into the hands of customers depends on what the event is. For some things, such as benefit performances or festivals, you'll probably sell the tickets at your place of business.

If you're giving away tickets, you can enclose them in personal invitations or direct mailings. They can be displayed on your counter or included in a trade show packet. Or you can give them away to the first 100 customers who come in on a given day or buy a particular product. If the tickets are for a fund-raising event at a local school, the students can take responsibility for selling them. No matter how they get out into the world, it's well worth the time to create and print tickets that will keep promoting your business, long after the event is over and forgotten. ■

MARKETING TIPS

◆ Take the time to create a memorable ticket

◆ Have prizes redeemed at your place of business

◆ Partner with another guerrilla to offer joint frequent buyer plans

◆ Conduct research to find the right target audience for the event

Customer research

Before sending out tickets to an event, it's a good idea to know which customers or prospects are most likely to be interested. Of course, if you're sending out party tickets, not much research is involved. But if you're asking people to enter a contest, attend a conference, or come to a lecture or demonstration, it's only good guerrilla thinking to cull out the hottest prospects.

The goal in customer research is not only to identify who your actual or potential customers are, but to find out what they do, what their desires and motives are, and what they are most likely to "buy."

The easiest and fastest way to get customer data is to ask questions. Your customers are the best source of information about how to improve your product or service, how and where to advertise, and how to run your business. Most people are flattered to be asked for their opinion. When your customers see that you're taking their suggestions and criticisms to heart, it will increase their desire to cooperate.

You don't need an expensive formal survey to begin your research. After you've identified the audience you'd like to poll, create a simple questionnaire. If possible, make it fun to fill out and offer a reward for doing so; perhaps a discount coupon or a prize when the questionnaire is returned.

Avoid leading and open-ended questions and keep the questions short. The most valuable questionnaires are those that ask questions that can be answered with a simple Yes or No and then provide space for a brief explanation. Here're some of the things to think about as you draw up your questions:

- Is there a need for your product? Find out if people already have your product or are happy with a substitute. These are straight-out questions: When did you last buy a television? How often do you purchase over-the-counter medications? Do you own a boat?

- What do you want to know about the prospects? You might ask about their occupation, education, or hobbies and exercise habits. Avoid demographic questions about income or marital status, although it's usually okay to inquire about children.

- What is the best way to reach your prospects? Do they read daily newspapers? Magazines? Use the Yellow Pages? How often do they shop in malls or specialty stores? Do they order items through the mail or from the Web?

- Who is the competition and what do they like or dislike about them? Be specific. For example, where do you currently bank? What is the best thing about your minivan? How could your copy center improve their service?

Duplicate, rotate, and flip selections

To use the Advanced tools on text, you must turn the text into a graphic. For complete instructions, see the "Change text into a graphic" how to in Reminders. (The Background preference in this file was set to a checkerboard pattern so that the white and transparent areas could be distinguished. See the Developing into a designer topic for more information on setting preferences.)

*This ticket example was created from scratch. To find the correct size for a ticket, a ticket template from Projects > Cards > Tickets was opened. Clicking on the memory size in the lower right of the window displayed the template dimensions. Using File > New, a file was created using these dimensions. **The text was entered, dragged into place, and deselected.** The file was then saved as a JPEG file. (Opening the JPEG file displayed the text on Layer 0 against the white background that is automatically created as part of a JPEG file.)*

The white area was selected using the Color Wand tool. The Add button was used to include the white areas inside of the letters in the selection.

239

The white areas were deleted using the Advanced > Edit > Delete tool.

The Invert button in the Selections palette was used to invert the selection so that just the letters were selected.

The text was duplicated using the Edit > Duplicate tool. The duplicated text appeared on Layer 1.

The text on Layer 1 was then dragged to the top of the ticket. (Make sure the pointer is black before you drag or resize the text.)

*The Rotate tab was clicked and the text was reselected using the Object Selection tool. (Clicking the Rotate tab deselects the text. **You must reselect the text after clicking the Rotate tab and before using a Rotate tool.** If you don't, all the text will rotate instead of just the text on the current layer.)*

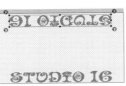

The Rotate Right tool was used to flip the text before it was resized and dragged into its final position.

The Edit tab was clicked and the text was re-selected using the Object Selection tool.

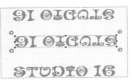

The Edit > Duplicate tool was used to duplicate the text again.

The Rotate tab was clicked and the text was re-selected using the Object Selection tool.

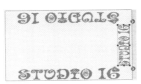

The Rotate Right tool was again used to flip the text which was then resized and dragged to the right side of the ticket.

The same steps were used to complete the border: 1) Click Edit tab 2) Select text 3) Click Duplicate tool 4) Click Rotate tab 5) Select text 6) Click Rotate Right tool 7) resize and drag into position.

Calendars

Marketing all year long

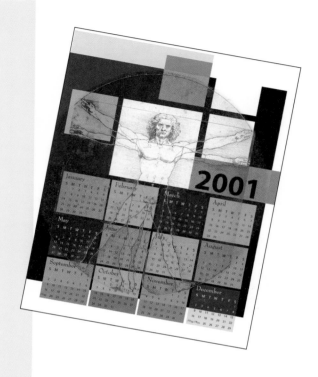

Calendars are an unobtrusive, user-friendly way to carry your marketing message right into your customer's home or office. A handsome, professional-looking calendar is a daily reminder of you and your company. It reflects your appreciation for the customer's business and reiterates that you're interested in building a long-term, reciprocal relationship.

Year calendars are quick to make but long on marketing value. This example uses the Wide/Side year template.

Creating a calendar

Before you decide to give calendars as gifts or premiums (or sell them as fund-raisers), you need to decide how much time, money, and energy you have to put into the project. For a quick promotional calendar, choose one of the year styles in the Projects > Cards > Calendars guided activity. On the year templates all the months appear on one page. Simply add your name, slogan, and logo, print on an attractive color stock, and you have instant gifts.

If you have more time and want to put in more effort, you can create a calendar with separate pages for each month. This type of calendar is more suited to the display of interesting photographs and subtle marketing messages. The photos can be of your company, your products, and your employees. Or choose nature, holidays, animals, or just about any other subject matter you want. It's always smart to match the photos to the desires and needs of your target audience. Keep in mind that you will need to have the pages bound in some way. Most copy centers will spiral-bind a calendar for very little cost.

Allowing time for production

When you produce a monthly calendar, you need time not only for design but also for printing. Depending on how big

Affinity marketing

Calendars are a good opportunity to engage in affinity marketing. Affinity marketing is like word-of-mouth, only faster. Like word-of-mouth, it depends on trust to work effectively.

Affinity marketing is the building and use of marketing partnerships. Simply put, it means that you and another business work together to offer your combined customers a deal that benefits both companies.

Co-marketing works best when both companies occupy the same niche or have the same target market. For example, you as a children's photographer might approach a children's clothing store and offer to do their advertisements for free. In exchange, they agree to include a coupon for your services in every customer package. The store gets beautiful, high-quality ads and you get lots of new prospects. Or, as the owner of a pizza restaurant you might trade discount coupons in conjunction with a local movie house. Both of you get increased business on Friday nights.

Because a calendar can be a lot of work and cost a fair amount of money, it's a natural for affinity marketing. Both businesses get out their message and save by splitting the cost. But affinity marketing lends itself to many other forms of guerrilla marketing as well: flyers, coupons, sponsorship, print ads, and inserts, just to name a few. Take a look around and you'll probably find a fellow guerrilla eager to take advantage of this joint marketing strategy.

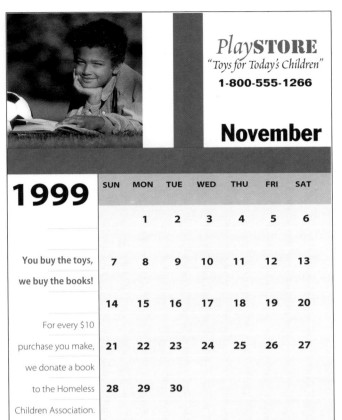

PlaySTORE
"Toys for Today's Children"
1-800-555-1266

November

1999

SUN	MON	TUE	WED	THU	FRI	SAT
	1	2	3	4	5	6
7	8	9	10	11	12	13
14	15	16	17	18	19	20
21	22	23	24	25	26	27
28	29	30				

You buy the toys, we buy the books!

For every $10 purchase you make, we donate a book to the Homeless Children Association.

◆ Design around the company's identity

◆ Go for maximum visuals and keep advertising discreet

◆ Match the visuals to your target audience

◆ Pre-punch holes to make hanging easier

Generating sales with calendars

In and of themselves, calendars are not sales generators but subliminal reminders. However, you can add a little something extra to your calendar, such as a monthly discount coupon, that will bring the customers into your store on a regular basis. You can even time the coupons so that they apply to seasonal sales or design them to reflect the photos for each month. If you're in the retail trade, including coupons in a calendar also makes it a more valuable gift for your customers to give to others. ■

a run you plan, you may find color xeroxing a reasonable alternative to printing each page individually. If you plan to give the calendars as year-end gifts, you must have them in hand by November at the latest. This means you probably need to start planning as early as August.

Word-of-mouth marketing

Nicely produced calendars are one of the best ways to generate that old-fashioned, but invaluable, commodity called word-of-mouth advertising. Some people tend to overlook the value of word-of-mouth recommendations.

While it's true you can't buy this kind of advertising directly, as you can an ad or a flyer, you can invest the time and money to increase word-of-mouth. What is commonly called word-of-mouth is often the result of effective print, radio, or direct mail marketing. Word-of-mouth can be a long time in coming. It's your years of hard work, quality products, honest service, and striving to create satisfied customers that will pay off handsomely in sincere word-of-mouth recommendations that continue for as long as you're in business.

There are many ways you can encourage word-of-mouth. Here're some simple ideas to get you started:

- Distribute your business cards far and wide. Include them in every mailing, post them on every bulletin board, hand them out at every meeting, and give several to every prospect and customer. Especially in the service industries, personal recommendations are your bread and butter.

- Give all your new customers marketing materials. Anything they take with them—ads, reviews, articles, brochures—will remind them of why they went to you in the first place and will encourage them to discuss you with others.

- Get your best customers to work for you. Supply your top customers with brochures that include a 10% discount for new customers. Then reward your loyal customers with a special bonus for every customer they bring in.

- Ask for it. Remind all your customers that you appreciate their business and referrals.

- Offer gift certificates. This is a convenient way for satisfied customers to spread the word.

- Do a great job. The single best way to generate great word-of-mouth is to knock the socks off your customers with extraordinary products and service. It's your own dependability and reliability that will make your customers want to share their experience of working with you with their friends.

Use blending modes

If you're feeling adventurous and want something special in your calendar creation, try playing with layer blending modes. Blending modes change the way that layers look when viewed together. For example, applying a mode may make part of a layer lighter or darker or turn it into a new color.

This calendar was created using the Tall/Above year template from the Projects > Cards > Calendars guided activity

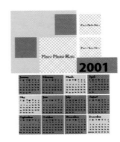

Since no photos were added to the template, the "Place Photo Here" text was selected and deleted

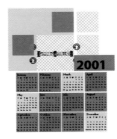

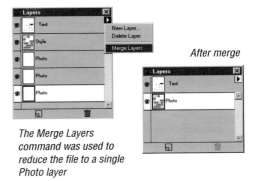

The Merge Layers command was used to reduce the file to a single Photo layer

After merge

The photo to be used in the calendar was opened

The photo was dragged from its own window into the calendar window and positioned

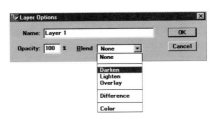

To experiment with different looks, the Photo layer was double-clicked in the Layers palette to display the Layer Options dialog box. Various modes were chosen from the Blend menu until the calendar had the desired look.

Here are some examples of effects you can get using blend modes

Darken mode

Overlay mode

Difference mode

Holiday cards

Partaking of the season

Joining in national holidays and celebrating with your customers and clients combines the best of two worlds. It allows you to both show appreciation for their business and honor the distinct historical and cultural backgrounds that make up your customer base.

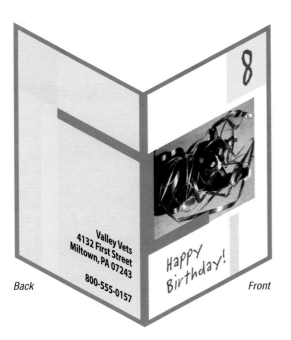

Back

Front

Inside
left

Inside
right

Personalized birthday cards show your customers you think of them as individuals. This card uses the hapybday template from the Projects > Cards > Holiday Cards guided activity.

Traditionally, the end-of-the-year holidays are the time to send out cards to your customers and clients. These cards not only serve to remind customers of your gratitude, they also allow you to personalize the sometimes monotonous nature of direct mailings. But greeting cards don't have to be limited to specific seasons.

Celebrating all kinds of holidays

Before the ease of desktop publishing, businesses often had a publishing company print their holiday greetings. This often resulted in very generic cards, chosen from whatever samples were available. With PhotoDeluxe Business Edition, you can not only create your own cards, but you can customize your cards to make them more personal.

DESIGN TIPS

◆ Be aware of cultural taboos and stereotypes

◆ Make the message and envelope as personal as possible

◆ Create individualized address labels

◆ Handwrite the message inside the card or sign each card individually

Note cards let your customers know you haven't forgotten them after their purchase

Both small and large card templates are available for general holiday greetings, Christmas, and Hanukkah. You'll find these templates in the Projects > Cards > Holiday Cards guided activity. But you can easily adopt these templates, or use the blank templates, to create more specialized cards. Design your own Kwanza or Felice Navidad cards. Celebrate with Chinese New Year cards. Send out cards for St. Patrick's Day or Columbus Day. Honor Memorial Day, Presidents' Day, and Labor Day with more than just sales. And, if you have the information in your database, it's a cinch to produce personalized birthday cards.

Sending out note cards

Cards don't need to be limited to holidays and special events. You can use greeting cards to remind customers that you're thinking of them (Hope you're enjoying your new stereo system, Just a note to says thanks again for the referral, Isn't it time to start thinking about a new car?). Or send a thank you card for a purchase at the one-month,

Marketing to specialized ethnic and demographic groups

One of the guerrilla rules of thumb is that profits are increased when you focus on a target market. Ethnic markets, by their definition, are made up of a natural target group. By positioning yourself within these groups, you can build a loyal following firmly based in the group's affinity for each other.

Any ethnic group resents a carpetbagger exploiting their market. You need to be very careful in the assumptions you make. Even if you're a member of the group, don't take things for granted. A good first step is to hire a consultant or agency to help you create an advertising plan, but you must also do your homework. Find out what cultural and personal values are esteemed by the ethnic group. Investigate the competition and the available ethnic advertising media. Above all, be genuine, listen to all feedback, and move slowly. Your sincerity and respect for your audience will do much to help spread the message, both through your positioned advertising and through word-of-mouth.

Ethnic groups are not monolithic. Don't insult the target audience by treating them as a homogenous unit. Of course, you are aware of the larger ethnic groups, such as Blacks, Hispanics,

and Asian-Americans. But did you know that there are smaller ethnic groups (Laotians and Puerto Ricans) or well-off cultural groups that are more demographic than ethnic (professional women or older citizens)? To find out more about your market, take advantage of the huge store of ethnic and demographic information available from the Bureau of the Census. Most of this data can be obtained at no cost.

To be successful in ethnic marketing, you must carefully delineate your target market, clearly define your product, and then use direct mail, direct response, and pinpointed advertising to reach your audience. Using these strategies, you can enjoy the success generated when a group expresses their appreciation with purchasing power.

MARKETING TIPS

- ◆ Use your database to pull out specific groups

- ◆ Allow enough time for delivery of time-sensitive cards

- ◆ Do your research when entering ethnic markets

- ◆ Send the note or card you'd like to receive from your suppliers

Back

Front

Inside
left

Inside
right

Recognize your customers' ethnic heritages by sending specialized cards. This card uses the hanukkah template.

six-month, or one-year anniversary of the sale.

Personal notes are also a good way to show you recognize a customer's needs and preferences. If you've collected the right information with your customer survey, you can notify customers of new products or services that they've expressed an interest in. You might also drop them a line to let them know that a new shipment of a personal favorite has arrived. The key is to keep the tone personal—

that's what distinguishes these mailings from the generic mail-merged variety.

Personalizing the envelope

Holiday cards and personal notes are not the time to used preprinted business envelopes with bulk-mail postage. Individual or small mailings present the perfect opportunity to produce unique return and address labels. Or decorate the envelope with an individualized sticker. Using appropriate commemorative stamps adds the final touch of individuality to these mailings. ■

Create a soft-edged collage

Collages can be fun and creative ways to individualize cards and other marketing materials. PhotoDeluxe Business Edition provides several diffferent ways to make collages. Here's how to create a simple collage combining a logo with a photo.

Two images were combined to create this collage

The Special Effects > Collage > Composites guided activity was used to bring together the photos for the collage. This activity places each photo on a separate layer.

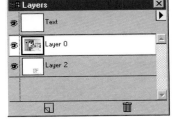

The layers were rearranged in the Layers palette so that the photo that was not going to be changed was on the bottom

To get a seamless effect where the photos blended, the Advanced > Tools > Eraser tool was used with a soft-edged brush

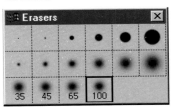

The top layer was erased to expose the underlying layer. When using the Eraser tool, it's best to use small strokes so that you can easily undo the last stroke with the Undo button.

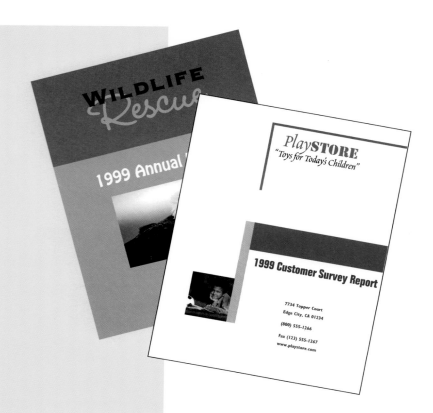

Report covers

Putting your best face forward

I n this age of video-conferencing and emailing, it's amazing how many reports still need to get written and distributed in printed form. Every business produces reports— from competitive analyses to feasibility studies, from marketing proposals to annual reports. One way to assure that your report gets read is to give it a customized and attractive cover.

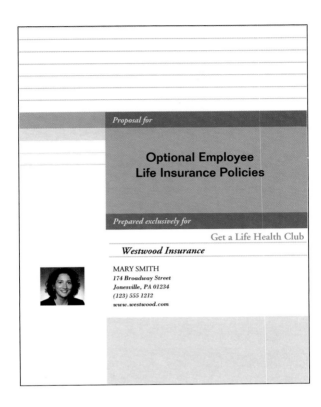

Creative use of color adds interest to this report cover, which uses template repcov05

Inside the cover image:

Proposal for

**Optional Employee
Life Insurance Policies**

Prepared exclusively for

Get a Life Health Club

Westwood Insurance

MARY SMITH
174 Broadway Street
Jonesville, PA 01234
(123) 555 1212
www.westwood.com

Internal reports

Today interdepartmental report summaries are often posted on internal Web sites. But when it comes to analyzing data and information, printed reports still rule. Whether you are the writer or the recipient, an informative and stimulating report cover makes a good impression. The main purpose of the cover is to state the report contents and indicate the date and the author. Adding photos or other graphics can help distinguish the

Making a commitment

Being a guerrilla marketer is sometimes a lonely job. There will be days when your best-laid plans go astray, when no one responds to your brilliant ad, when the computer crashes as you're updating your database. On the other hand, there will be days in which you thrill at being your own boss, your favorite customer makes a five-year deal to buy from you exclusively, and your clients call to express their gratitude and appreciation for your great service.

Guerrilla marketing may be relatively new, but it knows how to learn from history. The following was written by one Thomas Smith in London back in 1885. Use it as your guide each time you run an ad or get less of a response than you'd hoped for.

1. The first time a person looks at an ad, they don't see it.

2. The second time, they don't notice it.

3. The third time, they are conscious of its existence.

4. The fourth time, they faintly remember seeing it.

5. The fifth time, they read the ad.

6. The sixth time, they turn up their nose at it.

7. The seventh time, they read it through and say, "Oh, brother!"

8. The eighth time, they say, "Here's that confounded thing again!"

9. The ninth time, they wonder if it amounts to anything.

10. The tenth time, they ask their neighbors if they have tried it.

11. The eleventh time, they wonder how the advertiser makes it pay.

12. The twelfth time, they think it must be a good thing.

13. The thirteenth time, they think it might be worth something.

14. The fourteenth time, they remember that they wanted such a thing for a long time.

15. The fifteenth time, they are tantalized because they cannot afford to buy it.

16. The sixteenth time, they think they will buy it someday.

17. The seventeenth time, they make a memorandum of it.

18. The eighteenth time, they swear at their poverty.

19. The nineteenth time, they count their money carefully.

20. The twentieth time they see the ad, they buy the article.

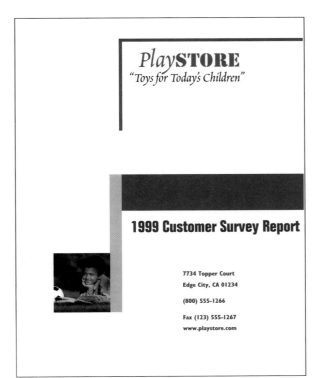

This playful design reflects the nature and products of the company. This example was created from template recov03.

Design Tips

◆ Create a cover that invites the audience to open the report

◆ Use white space to create contrast

◆ Use colored stock to increase interest

◆ Include all relevant information on the cover: title, author, date, company

---

contents and character of the report and provide a visual introduction to its contents. Even for your summary of customer responses, adding a little color or a photo can go a long way toward lightening difficult reading.

External reports

Reports from one business to another or from a business to its customers require a slightly different approach. Here the report cover helps to set the tone of formality and importance of the written data. Most often these covers will contain a company name and logo as well as a title and date. The color and style of the cover should reflect your marketing strategy and positioning. A cover on a marketing proposal for a million-dollar advertising campaign will probably differ significantly from the cover of a re-

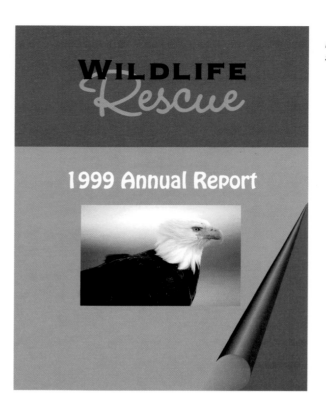

This elegant report cover is impressive in its simplicity

port on a weekend conference. The cover of "Tips for Investors" will have a different feel from a report on "The Beneficial Effects of Goldenseal."

Annual reports

One important public relations tool often overlooked by entrepreneurs is the annual report. Your annual report doesn't have to convey the same tone and information as the one sent to the stockholders of a Fortune 500 company. It doesn't have to be chock-full of tables with sales revenues and profits. Your report can simply provide information to your customers. Use it as an opportunity to be creative. You can discuss the results of your latest customer survey, explain a bit about your plans for the next year, or review your business goals and priorities.

No matter what kind of a report you're producing, you'll find a template to fit your needs in the Projects > Forms > Report Covers guided activity.

Why issue an annual report?

Probably one of the best results of issuing an annual report is the shock effect. BGM (Before Guerrilla Marketing), annual reports were the exclusive domain of the big guys. But desktop publishing has changed all that. Don't attempt to produce a full-color 30-page extravaganza. An inviting cover and a few well-laid-out pages of news, information, and photos are all that's needed. Don't forget to send a copy to the media and maybe you'll reap some free publicity while you're at it. ■

Create page curl

Page Curl

You can create an inviting report cover using the Special Effects > Cool > Page Curl guided activity. By default, this guided activity curls from the top to the bottom of the page. If you want to curl a smaller area, make a selection before applying the effect.

The first step of the guided activity lets you choose a color for the area under the curl.

In this example, a color was picked from the title section of the report cover so that the area under the curl would exactly match the rest of the cover.

Whenever you're choosing a color, you have the option to select a color from an open photo rather than clicking one of the color Swatches in the Color Picker. To choose a color from a photo, make sure the Color Picker is open then move the cursor over the area in the photo that contains the color you want to use (you'll see that the cursor becomes an eyedropper when you move it into a photo). Click the color in the photo and it appears as the Foreground color in the Color Picker.

When you want to curl a smaller area, select the area before clicking one of the directional curl buttons in the Page Curl step.

In this example, the Rectangle tool was used to select the lower right area of the photo before the Page Curl Right button was clicked.

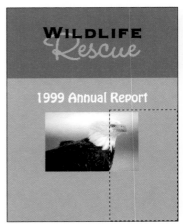

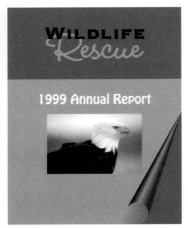

Where to go for more

This book introduces you to the concepts of guerrilla marketing and the uses of Adobe PhotoDeluxe Business Edition. In addition to this book, here are some sources for more information and resources.

More Guerrilla Marketing books:

Guerrilla Marketing
Guerrilla Marketing Attack
Guerrilla Marketing Weapons
The Guerrilla Marketing Handbook
Guerrilla Marketing Excellence
Guerrilla Advertising
Guerrilla Financing
Guerrilla Selling
Guerrilla Marketing Online
Guerrilla Marketing Online Weapons
The Way of the Guerrilla

More information about Guerrilla Marketing:

Call 800-748-6444

More information about Adobe:

www.adobe.com

More information about PhotoDeluxe Business Edition:

www.adobe.com/prodindex/photodeluxebe/main.html

Credits

Author
Kate O'Day

Cover & Book Design
Linda Tapscott/Spitting Image

Art Direction
Kim Isola/Adobe Systems, Inc.

Illustration & Production
Michelle-jean Waddell/Spitting Image

About the authors

Kate O'Day has been a writer and photographer for over 20 years. Her company, Kate O'Day and Associates, has provided instructional design and technical documentation for numerous clients including Adobe Systems, Apple Computers, Netscape Communications, Claris Corporation, and Macromedia. She has also authored books for Adobe Press, Hayden Books, and the Waite Group.

As a photographer, Kate has documented historical sites and ritual events around the San Francisco Bay Area. Recently, she has been photographing the changing face of Ireland. For more information about Kate O'Day and Associates and the Portraits of Ireland project, visit the www.koday.com website.

Linda Tapscott has been a graphic artist for 16 years. Her company, Spitting Image, has designed and produced projects for Adobe Systems, Fawcette Technical Publications, and *Apple International Magazine*. Linda was responsible for designing and creating the illustrations for the *Adobe Photoshop 3.0 User Guide* and is the coauthor of *The Amazing PhotoDeluxe Book*.

Linda is also a contemporary artist who combines her technological skills and exploratory fine arts creativity. Her works have been exhibited in numerous shows around the San Francisco Bay Area, including the Pacific Art League of Palo Alto and the Ohlone College Art Gallery. Linda's work can be seen on the Internet at: www.ltapscott.com.

Index

Index

270

Colophon

This book was designed and produced using Adobe PageMaker, Adobe Illustrator, Photoshop, Adobe PhotoDeluxe Business Edition and Adobe Type Manager on a Power Macintosh 7500/100. The typefaces used throughout the book are Sabon for the body text, Letter Gothic for headlines, and Helvetica Condensed for sidebars and captions. Adobe Acrobat and Exchange were used to create PDF files for proofing. Digital dye-sub proofs were used for final proofing.

Adobe Press books examine the art and technology of digital communications. Published by Macmillan Computer Publishing USA, Adobe Press books are available wherever books about computers or the graphic arts are sold.

275